AN INTRODUCTION TO ORATORY
# KHITABAH

AN INTRODUCTION TO ORATORY
# KHITABAH

ABDÜLHAKİM YÜCE

New Jersey

Copyright © 2013 by Tughra Books

Originally published in Turkish as *Konuşma Sanatı: Hitabet* in 2011

16 15 14 13    1 2 3 4

All rights reserved. No part of this book may be reproduced or transmitted in any form or by any means, electronic or mechanical, including photocopying, recording or by any information storage and retrieval system without permission in writing from the Publisher.

Translated by Ogulgozel Atakova

Published by Tughra Books
345 Clifton Ave., Clifton,
NJ, 07011, USA

www.tughrabooks.com

Library of Congress Cataloging-in-Publication Data Available

ISBN: 978-1-59784-315-7

Printed by
Çağlayan A.Ş., Izmir - Turkey

# CONTENTS

## UNIT 1
## DEFINITION AND KINDS OF ORATORY SKILLS

Definition, Significance, Purpose and Subject of Oratory ............................................. 3
Types of Oratory ........................................................................................................... 5
    Subjects of Oratory ................................................................................................. 5
    Forms of Oratory .................................................................................................... 7
    A Brief History of Oration .................................................................................... 11
Oratory Skills of Arabs ................................................................................................ 12
Oratory Skills of Turks ................................................................................................ 14

## UNIT 2
## SERMON AS A KIND OF RELIGIOUS ORATORY

Kinds of Religious Oratory .......................................................................................... 19
Religious Oratory inside the Sanctuary ....................................................................... 20
    Preaching and Sermons ........................................................................................ 20
    Principles of Sermons ........................................................................................... 22
    Conditions of Sermon Validity .............................................................................. 23
    *Sunnah*s of Sermons ............................................................................................ 25
    Abominable Points for Sermons ........................................................................... 26
    Supplications of Sermons ..................................................................................... 27
    Preparation and Presentation of Sermons ............................................................. 27
    Choosing a Subject ............................................................................................... 27

## UNIT 3
## BLESSED DAYS AND RELIGIOUS FESTIVALS

Religious Festivals and National Holidays .................................................................. 33
Blessed Nights ............................................................................................................. 37

Laylatul Mawlid ................................................................................................. 37
Laylatul Qadr .................................................................................................... 39
Laylatul Barat ................................................................................................... 42

## UNIT 4
## BEING AN IMAM AND MUEZZIN

Definition of Imam and Muezzin, and Their Importance and Position in History ........ 47
    Paying Wages to Imams and Muezzins ................................................... 51
    Duties of Imam and Muezzin .................................................................. 52
    Duties of Imam and the Preacher ........................................................... 53
    Duties of Muezzins ................................................................................. 53
    The Terms and Regulations of *Adhan* .................................................... 54

## UNIT 5
## RELIGIOUS ORATORY AND SUPPLICATION

Supplication ....................................................................................................... 59
Sermon Supplication ......................................................................................... 67
Recitations after the Daily Prayers .................................................................... 68
Supplication of *Adhan* ....................................................................................... 69
Salawat Munjiyah .............................................................................................. 69
Salawat Tafrijiyah .............................................................................................. 70
Sayyidu'l-Istighfar .............................................................................................. 70
The All-Beautiful Names of Allah ...................................................................... 71
Supplication of Food and *Iftar* (Fast-breaking Dinner) ...................................... 71
Supplication of the Sacrifice ............................................................................. 72
Funeral Supplications ....................................................................................... 73
Supplication of a Graveyard Visit ..................................................................... 75
Supplication of Recitation of the Whole Qur'an (Khatm al-Qur'an) .................. 75
Supplication of Marriage ................................................................................... 82

## READING TEXTS

Prophet Adam and Prophet Moses .................................................................. 85
The First Sermon .............................................................................................. 87
References ........................................................................................................ 89

# UNIT 1

## DEFINITION AND KINDS OF ORATORY SKILLS

# DEFINITION AND KINDS OF ORATORY SKILLS

**Definition, Significance, Purpose and Subject of Oratory**

Hitabet (a Turkish equivalent of "oratory") is a word of Arabic origin, which is used as a means of expressing one's necessities, reflections and causes. It has the following definition: "To direct one's words to another with the intent of explaining, delivering a sermon, uttering beautiful words, or preaching and counseling." As a term it means "a strong and effective speech, expressed with simple sentences and given to society to explain a certain purpose in a systematic, telic and methodical way in order to instruct, clarify, and preach, allowing the audience to consider a certain view as their own and to encourage certain actions." It can also mean "a beautiful eloquence, or ability to express words in a smart and smooth way; orating with ease and fluency." Words like "discourse," "speech," "address," etc. have the same meaning. A person giving a speech is called an orator; their speech is an oration.

Speech is a great asset to those who can use it well, but it can also be a wonderful weapon, too. One can please or hurt another person with language. A word can heal a broken house, or it can break a solid house. Masters of eloquence can inspire communities to have long contemplations. They can draw tears from a crowd, and they can change opinions, but they can also assert dominance over hearts and consciences. Word is a very effective way of connecting one soul's reflections to another's. Our noble Prophet is the most eloquent orator.

> Allah sends down in parts the best of the words as a Book fully consistent in itself" (az-Zumar 39:23); "And say to My servants that they should always speak (even when disputing with others) that which is the best. (al-Isra 17:53)

Allah the Almighty commanded to His Messenger: "*Say to them profound words that touch their very souls*" (an-Nisa 4:63). He gave directions to Prophets Moses and Aaron, peace be upon them, whom He sent to invite the Pharaoh to truth: "*But speak to him with gentle words, so that he might reflect and be mindful or feel some awe (of me, and behave with humility)*" (Ta-Ha 20:44). Our noble Prophet said: "Words have a magical power."[1]

The proverbs like "physical wounds heal faster than those caused by harsh words," and "good words are worth much and cost little, whereas harsh words are worth only loss," emphasize the importance of oratory. In fact, people of reflection, who can use oration and language as successful mediums, often gather many representatives around them and attain eternal existence for their concepts. Those who cannot orate or communicate effectively will likely disappear without a trace.

There is no specific subject of oratory; it may constitute any topic. Its desired subject may vary according to the necessities and conditions of an audience. Whatever its subject, it must inform, guide to a specific message, and entertain. In fact, these three essentials make up its purpose, too. The success of an oratory depends upon its outcome, i.e. directing people to useful action, whetting their desire to perform those good actions, and showing the dangers of not acting for good.

Oratory is comprised of three elements—the orator, the oration and the listener. Later on these elements will be explained in detail.

---

[1] *Sahih al-Bukhari*, Nikah, 47

## Types of Oratory

We may concisely investigate oratory, concerning its subjects and forms, under two basic headlines.

### Subjects of Oratory

If we consider oratory from the perspective of its subjects, there emerge many types. But if we consider oratory from the perspective of matters, four main types emerge. If to consider oratory from the point of view of its fields, then many kinds of it will emerge but if to fathom it from the point of view of matters, then there will appear four types of oratory:

**1. Military Oratory:** This is a kind of oratory used by commanders to excite and encourage soldiers. They are usually short and concise. These speeches must be quite short, but remain strong enough to be effective. The language must be acute, alive, brave, clear and open so that it can be understood by everyone. The purpose here is to help soldiers gain spiritual strength, and to provide them moral support. In battles, beside material and technical power, the most important element is a person's spirituality. One who is ready to die for his religion, nation, and home makes the best soldier. Good military elocution will help to inspire these feelings of pride. It can wipe away the fear of death by explaining the sacredness of being a war veteran or martyr. Oftentimes, examples from history are used to build fortitude.

The Holy Qur'an encourages holding military elocutions:

> O (most illustrious) Prophet! Rouse the believers to fighting. If there be twenty of you who are steadfast, they will vanquish two hundred; and if there be of you a hundred, they will vanquish a thousand of those who disbelieve. For they (the disbelievers) are a people who do not ponder and seek to penetrate the essence of matters in order to grasp the truth. (al-Anfal 8:65)

In the same way, our Prophet, too, has good examples concerning this. Here is one such example: "O People! Do not wish to confront your enemies! Do supplicate to Allah asking Him to keep you safe from calamities and tribulations. However, if you are to confront them, then have patience and know that Paradise is hidden under the shades of your swords."

After saying these motivational words, our Prophet went into his tent and supplicated to Allah in the form of plea: "O You, who sent the Book, who makes clouds move and is omnipotent to disrupt entire armies! Do disrupt them and be a helper of ours!"[2]

**2. Political Oratory:** These are convincing speeches, used by national leaders with the purpose of introducing themselves to the masses, and gathering people around their reflections and plans. They are called social oratories. In countries where parliaments are chosen democratically, oratory is performed in many mediums. Some of these places are the national Congress or Senate, party assemblies, voting locations, on radio or television, etc. In these speeches, politicians present their plans and projects for governing. If they are in the political opposition then they will try to explain things their opponents did not implement and tell about future improvements they would institute. Unfortunately, because of the retrogression of today's political life, there is often deceit, slander, and scandal in modern political oratory; as such, it has partially lost its persuasiveness. However, good political orators possess solemnity, steady character and trust.

**3. Judicial Oratory:** These are speeches narrated mainly in court by an accused person to defend himself, by an attorney to defend his client, or by a solicitor and complainant to accuse someone. The final cause for judicial oration is to distinguish between right and wrong. Some of these speeches, when given in defense of oppressed people or groups, can be exciting and sublime. Throughout history one can find unforgettable defense elocutions given in court rooms.

There are very beautiful and effective speeches of the Messenger of Allah, who said them not as a prosecutor but as a judge. Our mother Umm Salama, may Allah be pleased with her, narrated:

"Two men came to the Messenger of Allah and were making accusations about property, though neither man had proof or evidence. And the

---

[2] *Sahih al-Bukhari*, Jihad, 156

Messenger of Allah said to them: 'Both of you came to me because of a case. I am also a human being. It may happen so that one of you may explain the situation with its evidence much better than the other. As for me, I would give order to you according to your narrations. And in case I order to either of you an actual share of the other's property, then you should not accept it. For, that is a piece brought from Hellfire. And he will bring it as a burning fire in his hands at the Day of Resurrection.' After that there was a conversation between the brothers. With tears in their eyes, they both said: 'I devote that property to you, brother.' After which the Messenger of Allah uttered: 'If so, then go and divide out your property justly by casting your lots. Each of you take your share and then grant forgiveness to one another.'"[3]

Nowadays, when many illegalities are experienced, like the defense of unjust cases, the obfuscation of rational proofs, perjuries, bribing judges, and even the alteration of statements through duress, one may very rarely come across good legal elocution.

**4. Religious Oratory:** These are different kinds of speeches made by religious commissaries and pious scholars with the purpose of explaining religion. They are called religious oratory. Considering Prophet Adam was the first person and Prophet, he made religious speech the first kind of oratory. Thus it is the most important, wide spread oratory; to excel at it demands much knowledge, attention, and meticulousness. The greatest and sole duty of the Prophets was conveying the message of Allah, which could not be fulfilled without religious oratory. This is why it is considered to be the inheritance of the Prophets. In chapters to come we will give precise information on this kind of oratory.

## Forms of Oratory

There are different kinds of oratory concerning the forms of its narration:

**1. Oration (*Khitabah*):** Short and enthusiastic speeches uttered to listeners with the purpose of explaining some matter or reflection. As *khita-*

---
[3] *Sunan Abu Dawud*, Aqdiyya, 7:3584

*bah* is not expatiated, it is explained enthusiastically. Friday sermons of our noble Prophet were generally held in this way.

**2. Discourse (*Nutq*):** Explaining some reflection or feeling is called *nutq*. Political reflections and national causes are the main subjects. The intelligence and cultural understanding of listeners is not important.

**3. Conference:** A conference is any speech that elucidates scientific, philosophical or academic ideas. The intelligence of an audience is very important. Persuading the audience, exciting them, or leading them to activism is not the goal of a conference. Its purpose is to indoctrinate new ideas, inculcate certain truths and communicate one's discoveries concerning his discipline. Therefore, written form, excessive enthusiasm and strict expressions are not usually allowed. After the conference, the speaker might be asked questions from the audience, and might be demanded to provide further details and elucidations about his subject. Discussions about the ideas are very common.

**4. Talk (*Hasbihal*):** Subjects of talks may comprise all aspects of everyday life. They may vary from various opinions, events, and remembrances, to religious, scientific, and literary topics. Sometimes, one may explicate from a written paragraph. It is spoken in simple, comprehensible language with elegant, but witty expressions. Sometimes, the audience, too, may share their opinions or ask questions. Talks of our Prophet in mosques after the Morning Prayers represent the best examples of this kind of oratory. When the Prayer was over, he used to recite words of glorification and devotion until the sun rose to a certain point, and then he would turn to his Companions, cross his legs, and talk to them. In these talks many subjects that were necessary to humankind were discussed, concerning everyday matters, memories of the past, interpretation of dreams, and service to faith. He also answered questions, and comforted those who had problems. In other words, right after the circle of worship, the circle of scientific and spiritual knowledge was founded[4]. Here is the reason for founding such a circle of spiritual and scientific knowledge: Our Prophet did it for the sake

---

[4] *Sahih Muslim*, Masajid, 286; *Sunan Abu Dawud*, Salah, 301

of educating his Companions so they could give the same lessons to their successors. The founding took place when our Messenger decided not to be in touch with his wives for about a month. The next day, after saying his Morning Prayer and without reciting his daily glorifications, he went to the oriel named Mashruba. Everyone, and especially noble Umar ibn al-Khattab, realized that something important had happened. Indeed, there befell the event of *Ila* (separation of a husband from his wife for a certain period of time), which caused the revelation of some verses. From here it became obvious that these morning talks were to always be held. What could a person, who listened continuously for more than ten years to the morning talks of the Prophet have earned? We guess only those who experienced it would know it.

**5. Conversation:** An interactive discourse with two or three participants is called a conversation. It should comply with the spoken language and intelligence of its participants.

**6. Debate or Discussion:** An interactive conversation spoken according to common speech rules is called a discussion, whereas an interactive discourse between several people speaking for or against a certain view, by putting forward their own ideas, is called a debate. It is a discourse between thesis and antithesis performed in the presence of a referee. In a discussion, there is no anxiety or competition; however, in a debate, there is a real competition between ideas. Finding truth is the point of debates. Discussions have strong ideas and views rather than fancy words and bright sentences. Discussions bring up many truths. There are examples of debates and discussions held between the Prophets and their addressees in the Holy Qur'an[5]. Our Prophet narrated a discussion between Adam and Prophet Moses[6] held within the allegorical realm.[7] Our Prophet even had a long debate with a committee from Najran about Prophet Jesus.[8]

---

[5] See, Al-Baqarah 2:258; Ash-Shu'ara 26:18–34.
[6] See, "Reading Text: Prophet Adam and Prophet Moses"
[7] *Sunan Abu Dawud*, Sunnah, 7
[8] *Tabari*, III, 162

**7. Panel Discussion:** It is a talk-like discussion of a topic by several people in front of an audience. The purpose here is not to come to a certain decision but to introduce the subject from different perspectives and to put forward various views of it. There is a need of at least three or four participants for a panel discussion to be useful. Participants include a foreman and other speakers. In general, these kinds of discussions are made in small halls with no microphones. At the end of the discussion the audience may ask questions to the participants; they may also asseverate their reflections concerning propounded views. If the audience starts a discussion afterwards, then it will be considered a forum.

**8. Symposium:** A symposium is a series of talks made by different people on various aspects of the same topic during the same session. There will usually be 10 to 15 minute individual speeches delivered by at least three, and at most six, participants during a symposium. Unlike a debate, a symposium features a far more cordial, collective atmosphere. If earnest conversations about an issue develop, the symposium will be considered successful.

**9. Open Forum:** In terms of style, an open forum resembles a combination of a debate and a symposium. In this kind of open setting, broad social issues are usually discussed. Hence, only distinguished people are selected as participants.

**10. Tirade:** A tirade is a long speech, concerning a certain topic, usually marked by harshly censorious language.

**11. Monologue:** A monologue involves one person, telling mostly funny anecdotes to a crowded audience. It is sarcastic, and tackles both the good and bad aspects of life. Monologues tend to capture one person's character. Today, monologues are practiced by comedians.

**12. Dialogue:** It has the same traits as a monologue but is performed by two people on stage. Dialogue is not considered a discourse because it is defined as being a performance.

## A Brief History of Oration

Creation started with the one syllable word of *"kun"* (be), being thrown into the sternum of non-existence. It may also be called a Divine oration uttered to existence. Oratory started from the very moment the first person learned "speech and expressive power." The latter is the great quality that distinguishes man from other creatures. Through this power of speech, humans became vicegerents on Earth. In fact, the All-Merciful Allah taught the Holy Qur'an to all His creatures. However, He bestowed people with speech and expressive power, and through them the opportunity to comprehend and interpret His Book. Because He taught the Holy Qur'an to every creature of the Universe, all of them do offer Him glorifications. *"The All-Merciful. He has taught the Qur'an (to humankind and, through them, the jinn); He has created human; He has taught him speech"* (ar-Rahman 55:1-4).

Hence, if we say that the history of oratory started with the first person, it would be appropriate. As the major and only duty of the Prophets was communicating Allah's message, which could not be done without oratory, it becomes clear that the first person on the Earth was a Prophet. If you consider the history of Prophethood, then each of the Prophets made great oratorical efforts to invite people to truth. Some parts of these efforts are narrated in the Holy Qur'an. Conversations between Prophet Noah and his nation, Prophet Abraham and his father, Prophet Moses and the Pharaoh, and so on are examples of these orations. As these examples show it is inaccurate to claim that oratory was developed recently by other branches of art and science. These arts and sciences were seriously influenced by oration.

In fact, the history of oration goes all the way back to the 5th Century B.C. Records show that Corax of Syracuse, gave private lessons and wrote a book on oratory. Because Corax, in Greek, means "a crow," Islamic sources call it "Ghurab al-Khatib." His student, Tisias, also wrote a treatise concerning oratory based on Corax's principles. At that time, oratory was not only a branch of art, but also a profession with a good income. According to the city-state system of Greece, politicians needed to be good orators to successfully represent their home regions. To this end, public courses were opened, and itinerant orators offered private lessons. However, the purpose of their orations was not to bring listeners to the truth but to sophistically deceive them, in the hopes they would accept the orator's views. Therefore, they often used equivocation and evasion to avoid specifics. Such dishonesty created an epidemic of misguided concepts, empiricism, and a sophistical rationality. Socrates, Plato and Aristotle were three great philosophers of the ancient world, all of whom struggled against this dishonest mentality.

The famous *Rhetoric* of Aristotle is known by Muslim scholars as *Kitab al-Khitabah*. In the *Rhetoric*, he transposed the views of late and contemporary orators, and then added new dimensions to the art by applying logic to it. In this respect, his work is the oldest and the most systematic treatise on oratory. *Rhetoric* was translated into Arabic several times and was annotated by many people.

For the first time in the history of Islamic culture it was pointed out by Al-Kindi that the equivalent of the word "rhetoric" was "balaghah." In Arabic literature, as oratory was related to *balaghah*, it was evaluated along such literary disciplines as meaning, speech, wonder, and the beauty of words. This is why logicians after Ibn Sina did not place it in their treatises.

## Oratory Skills of Arabs

**The Age of Ignorance:** It is known that Arabs placed great importance on oratorical skill. Before Islam, there were many famous Arab orators. In the presence of our Prophet, orators of different tribes used to give speeches. Tribal life and its conflicts tended to inspire the speakers. Hence, the subjects of their oratories proceeded accordingly. One of the main topics of oratory of the Age of Ignorance was mutual praise and satire. The richest examples of oratory in the Age of Ignorance comprise vengeful speeches uttered at battles between tribes. That said, there were also orations of reconciliation, and calls for peace. Many of these speeches were given at engagement and wedding ceremonies; they were called *khutbatu'l-imlaq*. According to old Arabic customs, a person with strong oratory skills among the kith and kin of a groom would expound on the groom's virtues; a member of the bride's family would reply in kind. A speech given by Abi Talib ibn Abdul Muttalib, at the marriage of our Prophet to Khadija, presents one of the finest examples of this kind of oration.

Other kinds of oration in the Age of Ignorance included speeches given at delegate receptions and assemblies of rulers, as well as those given at street fairs and various meetings. Words of predictors bearing information from the unseen were also common orations during the Age of Ignorance.

**Islamic Era:** Due to stylistic developments, Islam, from its earliest days, vastly improved the quality of oratory, and raised plenty of masters of *balaghah*. One of the major reasons for such an improvement was a renewed demand for this branch of art due to the debates between those spreading the Prophet's message of truth, and its dissidents. The quick spread of Islam led Arabs to develop in political and social ways. This increased the significance of oratory. The Prophet's persuasive and influential orations helped to invite many people to the truth of Islam. The first and the most substantial example of our Prophet's oratorical prowess was his speech given only to his tribesmen at the hill of Safa during the first years of his Prophethood.

Though some of his speeches are filed in fragments in the Hadith and Siyar Collections, many essential speeches of the Messenger reached our time. This shows the huge importance attached to oratory in Islam's earliest days. In sermons, our Prophet called people to forsake paganism and other kinds of beliefs common in the time of Ignorance. He invited the whole of humankind to Islam, which would lead them from darkness to light. He explained the beauties of Islamic credos, ways of attaining happiness in this world and in the Hereafter, and the virtues of jihad (striving in Allah's cause and for humanity's betterment). His speech given at the time of His Farewell Pilgrimage from the back of his camel to a hundred thousand people was comprised of such basic topics as faith in Allah, respect for human rights (especially protecting the rights of women), protecting brotherhood and sisterhood by strengthening bonds of religion, the equity of all people, and the significance of living according to the Holy Qur'an and the elevated Sunnah.

When delegates that came from different tribes discoursed with the noble Prophet, he used to ask his Companions to reply on his behalf. The most prominent among them was Thabit ibn Qays al-Ansari, who was known as a "speaker of the Prophet." After the death of the Messenger of Allah, Abu Bakr gave a speech concerning the candidacy of caliphs, which is considered to be an example of the first Islamic political oratory.

The Age of Happiness and the period of the Rightly-Guided Caliphs was the golden age of Arabic oratory. The great orators of that time were, first of all, our Prophet, then Ali ibn Abi Talib, other caliphs, the commanders of armies, and governors. At their appointed places, governors would gather people to that area and give speeches concerning their plans of action.

Oratory was weakened by the imperialism of non-Arabic nations. In particular, as the written word spread, oratory was replaced by letters and imperial edicts. With the passage of time, oratory was delivered exclusively at Friday and religiously festive sermons, and also during wedding ceremonies.

## Oratory Skills of Turks

The words of Bilge Khagan (8$^{th}$ Century) written on Orkhon inscriptions show that the custom of Turkish oratory has roots deep in history. However, besides Bilge Khagan, we have little knowledge concerning the four or five centuries after him. In the book of *Kutadgu Bilig*, a treatise from the 11$^{th}$ Century, there are explanations of subjects like language, the power of language, and its peculiarities, advantages and disadvantages. Despite this book, it is not easy to capture specifics about Turkish oratory. Another book, *Atabat al-Haqaiq*, a 12$^{th}$ Century treatise, was a book of preachment, but it contains no information concerning oration. At the same time, this treatise was clearly written to meet society's need for guidance, and it contains all the necessary information for preachers.

Multiple factors ensured a plenitude of ceremonial orations in Turkish social life. Many nations comprised Turkish culture, and this meant there were many different ceremonies and occasions for oration: weddings, name-giving ceremonies, the taking of oaths and so on. Many examples of these orations have reached us through the stories of Dede Korkut. He was described as a "wise, educated and strong poet, who was supremely gifted at language and poetry." Through his work, we know that in Turkish society people like shamans, saints, the *bakshy,* and others acted as orators at ceremonies.

A branch of religious oratory known as pulpit oratory has very old roots in the governance of the Turkish state, and also other Islamic states. Preaching, which was regarded as an independent occupation in Ottoman society, was turned into an establishment. There came to be an academic status the highest rank of which was the sheikhdom of Ayasofya (Hagia Sophia) pulpit, where talented silver-tongued sheikhs of Sufi lodges were appointed to. The prominent 12$^{th}$ Century Sufi, Ahmad Yasawi, headed the first significant branch of preachers.

In the area of Turkish military oratory, Alp Arslan, the great ruler of the Seljuk Dynasty, was the first recorded commander. His speech before the battle of Malazgirt is one of unforgettable examples of Turkish military oratory. Speeches that function as political testament are quite good at being sincere, brief, and impactful.

Even in our times, the Turkic population has raised numerous great orators and they have given us many examples of beautiful and influential military, political and religious oratories.

## ASSESSMENT

1. Write the kinds of oratories according to subjects.
2. What time can we refer to as the beginning of oratorical history?
3. Write about the oratorical skills of pre-Islamic Arabs.
4. What is symposium?
5. What is talk?

# UNIT 2

## SERMON AS A KIND OF RELIGIOUS ORATORY

# SERMON AS A KIND OF RELIGIOUS ORATORY

## Kinds of Religious Oratory

Religious oratory is a speech given by religious officials or those who received a religious education. In short, it is an oration delivered to a community by a specialist with the purpose of clarifying and explaining religious truths. Here are three points that should be paid attention to:

1. A person who delivers a religious oration should be a specialist in that field. If religious oration is delivered by someone without enough education, it is possible they could use their address to distort and manipulate. Religious leadership requires serious spiritual responsibility. A lack of education among religious leaders and orators is a major factor in the spiritual chaos of our time. .

2. The place and environment where a religious oration occurs is also important. A speech that aims to be serious and peaceful, that aims to unite people and please Allah, cannot be delivered just anywhere; the wrong environment will bring harm rather than benefit. Despite this, our Prophet used to find any opportunity, in any place, to talk about to his community about the truth. Unfortunately, the situation has changed since then. Some speeches, which are delivered via TV programs, panel discussions or conferences, are prone to creating discord. In such an environment, where the

audience is not serious and often reckless, it can be difficult to tell about the truth. Religious oratory must be performed at sanctuaries and sacred places, or in celebration of certain ceremonies.

3. Oratory must include religious topics only. In other words, it should be done to announce truths of religion. People that deliver their message with arrogance, initiate social propaganda or racial discrimination and dissent, who bring to their agenda only controversial subjects—in short, those who speak about matters other than religion—would not be considered as having delivered religious oration.

Religious oratory can be given anywhere, but is most fulfilling in places of worship. However, it is well approved to separate the subject into two basic groups "inside the sanctuary" and "outside the sanctuary" to better explain and understand the matter.

## Religious Oratory inside the Sanctuary

### Preaching and Sermons

*Khutba* (sermon) is a word of Arabic origin, which means, according to the dictionary, an emphatic speech in which one addresses people, speaks to them, and convinces them. As a term, it is a religious talk that consists of an introduction and admonition performed at certain times and places, and is propounded by authorized people. *Khutba* is remembrance and worship as well as preaching and lesson.

*Khatib* (preacher), which is derived from the same root as *khutba*, is a person who propounds a sermon to a community from the pulpit of a mosque. In Turkey, the term "imam-*khatib*" is used. A person obliged with that duty delivers sermons and leads the *salah* (the Daily Prayers). In the past, and especially in big mosques, different persons used to deliver sermons and lead Prayers. A preacher used to be appointed by the head of the state (i.e. *padishah* for Ottomans); those, who did not have a permission slip (Certificate of Oratory) could not deliver sermons. Nowadays, the duty of appointment is undertaken by the Presidency of Religious Affairs on behalf of the President of Republic.

The first sermon was read by our Prophet during his emigration from Mecca to Medina, at the mosque of Quba. In that sermon was the following revelation:[9]

> O you who believe! When the call is made for the Prayer on Friday, then move promptly to the remembrance of Allah (by listening to the sermon and doing the Prayer), and leave off business (and whatever else you may be preoccupied with). This is better for you, if you but knew. (al-Jumu'ah 62:9)

*Khutba* was considered as an obligatory act before Friday Prayers because of the expression "remembrance of Allah" mentioned above. Since then, Friday Prayers, performed without *khutba* are not considered to be authentic. Sermons should be read before Friday Prayers but after the Eid Prayers, and Prayers for rain and solar eclipses.[10] Some pious scholars state that, firstly, sermons were read after Friday Prayers, and they were brought forward only after the revelation of the 11th verse of the chapter of Al-Jumu'ah. They quote such an event: Once on Friday, in Medina, while our Prophet was delivering a sermon, drumbeats, informing people of the arrival of trade caravans, could be heard. As soon as they heard it, some members of the community just left the mosque in order to get their groceries. Thereupon, the following verse was revealed:

> Yet (it happened that) when they saw (an opportunity for) business or pastime, they broke away for it and left you standing (while preaching the sermon). Say: "What is with Allah is better (for you) than pastimes and business. Allah is the Best to be sought as the ultimate provider." (al-Jumu'ah 62:11)

After that event, sermons were delivered before the Prayer.

From the given verse it becomes quite clear that sermons are not to be abandoned—not for trade or any other reason. Consequently, from the first *adhan* (call to Prayer) of Friday Prayer till the ending of Friday *fard* (obligatory) Prayer, one needs to cease all kinds of commercial affairs.

---

[9] See, "Reading Text: The First Sermon"
[10] Before the Prayer of solar eclipse, sermons are delivered only in Shafi school.

Of this, here is a verse:

> O you who believe! When the call is made for the Prayer on Friday, then move promptly to the remembrance of Allah (by listening to the sermon and doing the Prayer), and leave off business (and whatever else you may be preoccupied with). This is better for you, if you but knew. When the Prayer is done, then disperse in the land and seek (your portion) of Allah's bounty, and mention Allah much (both by doing the Prayer and on other occasions), so that you may prosper (in both worlds). (al-Jumu'ah 62:9–10)

Our Prophet delivered his sermons in the language of the Holy Qur'an and his mother tongue, Arabic. As there was no disclosure on the possibility of sermons being delivered in other languages, I believe that sermons on general Islamic culture were comprehensible enough so that, until recently, Muslim non-Arab nations used to deliver sermons entirely in Arabic. During the years of the Turkish War of Independence, sermons partially started to be delivered in the Turkish language. Such patriot preachers like Mehmet Akif invited people to support the War of Independence through their sermons and their use of their native language. Since February the 3rd, 1928, sermons, preaching, and exhortations officially started to be delivered in the Turkish language. And today all sermons in mosques are given in Turkish.

## Principles of Sermons

According to Imam Azam Abu Hanifa, the basic element of a sermon consists of remembering Allah the Almighty. If one says *"Alhamdulillah"* (all praise be to Allah), *"subhan Allah"* (glory be to Allah) or *"La ilaha illa'llah"* (There is no deity but Allah) with an intention of delivering a sermon, then he will be considered to have delivered a sermon. However, according to Imam Abu Yusuf and Imam Muhammad's principles, a sermon should consist of perpetual remembrance and supplication, the length of which should at least be equal to *at-tashahhud* (the final section of *salah*); namely, the supplication of *al-tahiyyat* (benedictions) or three verses of any chapter of the Holy Qur'an. *Fatwa* (religious-legal responsum) and their implementations are done accordingly.

According to Imam Malik, sermons should bear glad tidings and warnings. To him, that is the principle of a sermon. As for Imam Shafi, there are five elements of sermons:

1. Praising the Almighty Allah in both sections of a sermon.
2. Invoking peace and blessings to our Prophet in both sections of the sermon.
3. Recommending *takwa* (the conscious performance of good and avoidance of evil).
4. Reciting a verse from the Holy Qur'an in either section of the sermon (reciting it in the first section is more virtuous).
5. Uttering supplications to believers in the second section of a sermon.

The principles of the Hanbali school, except for the last point, are identical to those of the Shafi school.

## Conditions of Sermon Validity

There is a need of certain conditions for sermons to be authentic. In each school of law there are some differences concerning conditions of validity. Awareness of those conditions and accomplishing them accordingly are very important for members of schools in light of their worship.

For the Hanafi school there is a need of these conditions:

1. Sermons should be delivered within the Prayer time.
2. Delivering sermons before the Friday Prayer.
3. Delivering sermons with an intention of preaching.
4. Delivering sermons to a community. In order to fulfill the last condition and make the sermon authentic, there is a need of the presence of at least one person besides the preacher. On the other hand, for the validity of sermons, a community does not have to listen; they only need to be present.
5. In the period between sermon and Prayer, do not engage in any activity, like eating, that is ill suited to the Prayer and sermon.

Purification from minor impurities, covering private parts and delivering the sermon in a standing position are not considered as conditions for sermon validity. However, one needs to adhere to them. For, according to the approved view, not only were these among deeds of the noble Prophet, there are pious scholars who state that they are incumbent to how a Muslim acts.

According to the Maliki school the following are conditions for the Friday sermons:
1. Preachers must deliver sermons in a standing position.
2. Both sections of the sermon should be delivered in the time of the Noon Prayer.
3. Both sections of the sermon should have contents of sermon.
4. Sermons should be delivered in mosques.
5. Sermons should be delivered before the Friday Prayer.
6. Sermons should be delivered before a community of, at least, ten people.
7. Sermons should be read clearly.
8. Sermons should be delivered in Arabic language.
9. Not to engage oneself with anything else in the period between the sections of the sermon, and between the sermon and the Prayer itself. As for Malikis, preachers are not obliged to have ablutions or intention before delivering sermons.

According to the Shafi school the following are necessary conditions for sermons to be valid:
1. All five principles of sermons must be fulfilled in Arabic language.
2. Sermons should be delivered in the noon time hour.
3. Preacher should deliver sermon in standing position if he is strong enough.
4. Preacher should sit between the two sections of a sermon if he has no excuse.
5. Elements of sermons should be heard by a community of at least forty people.
6. Sermons should be delivered before the Prayer. One should not occupy oneself with anything else both between sections of the sermon, and in the period between the sermon and the Prayer itself.

7. Preachers should be pure from major and minor impurities.
8. Preacher should comply with covering the private parts of his body.
9. Preacher must be a man.
10. Preacher should lift his voice enough in order to be heard by forty people.
11. Preacher should also function as a reliable imam if needed.
12. Preacher should possess at least some knowledge of differentiating between *fard* and *sunnah* parts of Prayers, or, at least, he should know that obligatory things are not *sunnah*. In the Shafi school, too, there is no need of intention for starting sermons.

## *Sunnahs* of Sermons

1. Preacher should be close to a pulpit in order for him to reach it easily without disturbing anyone. This is why he should perform his first *sunnah* Prayer of the Friday Prayer by the pulpit. Not adhering to this—in other words, his praying the *sunnah* Prayer somewhere away from *mihrab* or pulpit—is abominable.
2. Seating of preacher on the pulpit in a position with his face turned towards the community and reciting *adhan* in that position.
3. *Adhan* should be recited in the presence of preacher.
4. After *adhan* preacher should stand up and deliver his sermon in that position. There is an opinion that delivering the sermon on one's feet is mandatory.
5. Preacher should face the community while delivering his sermon.
6. After quietly saying "A'udhu-Basmala" (it is the Arabic expression of *A'udhu billahi min ash-shaytanirrajim. Bismillahir-Rahmanir-Rahim*. It means "I seek refuge in Allah from Satan eternally rejected (from Allah's mercy). In the Name of Allah, the All-Merciful, the All-Compassionate"), preacher should start the sermon by uttering, aloud, praises and glorifications to Allah the Almighty.
7. Preacher should say the Word of Testimony and invoke peace and blessings to our beloved Prophet.

8. Preacher should give advice to believers.
9. Preacher should recite a verse from the Holy Qur'an with an expression of "A'udhu-Basmala."
10. Sermons should be delivered in two sections in between which the preacher should stop for a three-verse-term length.
11. The preacher should start the second section of the sermon just like the first section: with praises and glorifications to Allah the Almighty and invocations of peace and blessings to the noble Prophet.
12. In the second section, the preacher should utter supplications to Allah in order for Him to grant forgiveness to believers, bestow upon them contentment and well-being, and make them victorious in their pursuits.
13. Preacher should utter the second section of the sermon with a lower voice in comparison to the first section.
14. Sermons should not be prolonged.
15. Sermons should be heard well by the audience.
16. Before the sermon, the preacher should have an ablution. His intimate parts should be covered. It is also asserted that these are mandatory acts.
17. After the sermon *iqamah* should be recited to start the Friday Prayer.
18. The preacher who delivered the sermon should lead the Friday Prayer.

Many points that Hanafi school agrees to as *sunnah* of sermons, Shafi school relates them to conditions of sermon validity.

## Abominable Points for Sermons

It is abominable to forsake the *sunnah*s of sermons. Talking or admonishing someone else while the preacher delivers a sermon is strongly reprehensible. Even the preacher replying to questions of the community concerning religious matters is not welcome, as our Prophet narrated certain principles regarding this, fearing that breaking these principles may bring disorder to a mosque's discipline. The audience should not distract their attention from listening to sermons. A person's greeting others or his returning others' greetings is also abominable. And even when the name of the Prophet is mentioned, listeners should either remain quiet or invocate peace and blessings to him with a low voice. Performing a Prayer during sermon is abominable, as well. However, according to the Shafi school, the Prayer of greeting the mosque may be lightly performed during a sermon.

## Supplications of Sermons

Alongside the Arabic component of sermons, there are certain supplications that a preacher must recite while ascending to the pulpit. Texts of supplications are given in the following sections.

## Preparation and Presentation of Sermons

Here we may mention three stages of preparing for a sermon: choosing a subject, preparing and presenting it.

## Choosing a Subject

A sermon is described as "teaching basics of religion, to an attentive community of wide and different cultural levels, in a considerably short time; or, if there is a need to, explaining from the Islamic point of view all positive and negative events or improvements that took place in that week's agenda and to elucidate these developments to people." The seriousness of choosing a proper topic becomes clear. For,

- sermons are delivered just once a week;
- the duration of sermons is short;
- the community belongs to different cultures, and includes both individuals of higher education individuals who are illiterate;
- since sermons are delivered on a Prophetic station and inside a place of worship, inappropriate topics are not to be spoken there, etc.;
- the pulpit is an important place, where one has a great opportunity to tell about the right way and the truth.

Under such circumstances, in order for the subject of a sermon to be effective, it must be precisely chosen and prepared from a list of the most necessary matters expected to confront the community that week. Because of the prevalence of media, many topics of state agenda are already widely discussed; hence, it may not be appropriate to deliver sermons on the same subject for the communities of all mosques. Preachers must pay attention to whom, where and with what purpose they will preach. Once they answer these questions, it should be quite clear to them what to speak about. Choosing a topic a community needs indicates the educational level and spiritual intellect of a preacher; it is his duty to educate his community.

Being persistent in reading his old sermons will prevent the preacher from boring his community be revisiting similar themes and subjects. Rehashing old lessons does not help a community acquire the spiritual and Islamic knowledge it needs to thrive in the world. Besides, revisiting old material will mean the preacher has not fulfilled the duties of his position. Sometimes, it may happen that a sermon prepared at the beginning of the week may be changed upon suddenly developing events.

After determining the subject of the sermon, there comes the most important part—planning the text. For, the worst plan is much better than having no plan at all. The following advice works for planning any kind of sermon:

**Expression of address:** One can refer to the community either as "Venerable Muslims," "Dear brothers and sisters in faith," or "Dear community."

**Telling the subject of the sermon:** To engage the community in listening, it is important to tell the determined subject of the sermon. One should not do this only by telling the name of the subject; it would be much more useful if he says with which purpose and from which dimension the given subject will be approached, and sometimes it would be much better to start the sermon not by stating its subject, but with an attention-grabbing sentence.

**Introduction:** It is important to make the introduction skillful in order to motivate the community to listen carefully. This could be done in the form of a question, telling about some event as an example, the reason of revelation within a verse, the reason a *hadith* emerged, the relation of a current subject to the community, or greatly emphasizing the significance of the subject.

**Progression:** In this section, examples from verses of the Holy Qur'an, *hadith*s of the Prophet, life styles of his Companions, and historical events should be given. It is necessary to express interpretations of them. Also, here information will be given about the conclusion, if there is one.

Conclusion: A brief summary of the subject could be given; a relevant verse or *hadith* could be recited, and ended with a supplication.

## ASSESSMENT

1. Explain religious oratory.
2. Where and in what conditions are sermons delivered?
3. How are sermons delivered? Elucidate their basics.
4. Under which conditions would sermons not find the right niche?
5. Write two verses, and their meanings, from the Holy Qur'an that tell about Friday Prayers.

# UNIT 3

## BLESSED DAYS AND RELIGIOUS FESTIVALS

# BLESSED DAYS AND RELIGIOUS FESTIVALS

## Religious Festivals and National Holidays

A holiday is a day of joy and bliss. It can be celebrated individually or collectively. It can be a day which is considered to be religious in nature, or a day which was very important to a nation's history.

National holidays are celebrated in cities and towns, and commemorate important historical moments in a nation's history. Usually, such days as Independence Days, Victory Days, or days of gaining human rights and significant administrative acquisitions, are declared national holidays. On these days, set aside to celebrate economic and military developments, there will often be different kinds of pageantry: military parades, public speeches, and the recitation of poems. It is not uncommon for folklore activities and sporting contests to be organized. Of course, other activities, depending on a country, may take place, too.

Among the holiday speeches, there will usually be some religious orations given, too. The emphasis in these orations will be national unity, but from a religious perspective. For example, if it is an Independence Day celebration, then supplications will be uttered to Allah the Almighty in order to not face bondage again. Speeches must be short, unifying, and bear features of historical consciousness. Religion, as one of a nation's most important elements, must be particularly emphasized. Certainly, according to conditions, topics of martyrdom and veteran care could be addressed.

Every religion and every nation celebrates religious holidays, too. Many nations' religious festivals are celebrated like their national holidays. Because there are few vestiges of religion remaining, these festival days have become days of entertainment. The level of excitement experienced during these festivals is well-proportioned with people's moral values. For example, the celebrations of some carnivals are today interpreted as days to "collectively release tensions and pour out one's feelings," and they have turned to the delirium of entertainment.

As for Islam, even on festive days, which are considered to be days of amusement and relaxation, the highest priority is given to drawing near to Allah and asking forgiveness. According to Muslims, festivals are periods of time that, despite their shortness, are kept in the heart, with inspirational blessings, goodness, benedictions and joy, for weeks and even months. During festivals there is such an abundance of extra favor and surprise gifts from the All-Just-Allah that could not be attained by any one man in ten days, a month, or even several years. In fact, all good deeds and benevolences will gain value only by turning to Allah. Festivals are the most significant means of Divine favor. Simply, it is a time to receive the boundless Divine grace that will sweeten our entire lives.

Surely, such an achievement will only be attained by those, who, if it is a case of *Eid al-Fitr* (a festival celebrated after the holy month of Ramadan), gave their dues during Ramadan and did not behave heedlessly on the day of festival. It is quite difficult to receive Divine gifts for those who spend religious festival days as if they were on vacation: by snarfing down all sorts of foods as if taking revenge for their month of fasting, and reverting to sins that they refrained from only temporarily. Only those who keep their circumspection and caution during festivals, just like they did during the month of Ramadan, who stand aloof from prohibited things their entire lives who have the mental capacity and perception of servanthood, will attain favors and benevolence in such a short time. For them, *Eid al-Fitr* is an inheritor of the holy month of Ramadan. In other words, whatever was promised in Ramadan on behalf of Divine rewards, will be given in *Eid al-Fitr*. Then, it is possible to possess the same fruits (of your work). Just as the Night of Destiny and Power squeezes so much in the way of favors and rewards, festivals, too, have the same quality.

The festival of *Eid al-Fitr* does not mean completely breaking from the month of Ramadan by leaving the days of fasting in the past, and practicing a freedom of contentedly eating and drinking. It is about the exhilaration of accomplishing the duties of servitude and hope, and through these duties, attaining the forgiveness of Allah the Almighty. A believer celebrates a festival not for leaving the days of fasting behind, but for having earned emancipation from the burden of his errors and sins. For, the festival is set up upon a complete appraisal of the Noble Ramadan, the beginning of which is a mercy, the middle forgiveness, and the ending salvation from Hell, and the vastness of Allah's mercy.

It does not, however, mean that at the end of fasting we get all the promised presents at once. First of all, the festival is joy. Secondly, Allah said: "Fasting is for Me, and I will give the reward for it."[11] Such a reward will be possible in the Hereafter only.

As for *Eid al-Adha* (Festival of Sacrifice), it bears remembrance of the fact that Prophet Abraham, peace be upon him, wanted to sacrifice his son Ishmael, peace be upon him, to which Ishmael agreed. Finally, Allah the Almighty, as a reward to the great fidelity of Abraham, sent an animal (sheep) for the act of sacrifice. Believers, by giving an animal as a sacrifice, experience the pleasure of these two great Prophets, successfully fulfilling Allah's command. Pilgrims, especially, experience even greater excitement during this festival by sharing this remembrance with others.

On the other hand, as mentioned above, Islamic festivals are very different from those of other cultures' carnivals and celebrations. The rebellion and mental alienation are never seen in the behavior and attitude of believers. There is the seriousness of being woken to and obeying the Holy

---

[11] *Sahih al-Bukhari*, Sawm, 2

Qur'an in balanced actions and dignified behavior. As usual, on festivals and in ordinary days, they will always stand by Allah and the Prophet. Their relations with others will be based upon respect, love and compassion. They will try not to waste even a single moment of festival days.

At the age of our Prophet there were no vacations for festival days. Those days were welcomed, in comparison to other ordinary days, much differently with Eid Prayer and a sermon. Later, they used to exchange smiles with one another, take care of the poor and give food to kith and kin. However, nowadays, festival days have elements of local customs, too. For example,

- the presence of vacations spared for festive days;
- importance will be attached to visiting graveyards;
- visiting relatives for the sake of maintaining bonds of kinship, or inquiring after their health via phone will provide a special profundity to festivals;
- relations between parents and children will be strengthened once more;
- such places like nursery schools and community dwellings, where there are people who suffer the misfortune of being alone, are visited and heartened. In doing so, somehow, one maintains bonds of kinship in a broader meaning of the word.

Taking into account the peculiarities of festivals and their place within a religion, festival speeches should be prepared. As festive speeches consist of preaching and sermons, elements, mentioned in the section of "Preaching and Sermons" should be recalled. Generally, one of the basic principles of Islam—like faith, worship or morality—is chosen as a topic of festive speeches. By considering the presence of certain people that come to mosque only on festival days, the subject will be discussed in a persuading and pleasing style. The purpose of a festival speech is to draw addressees' attention to the topic and to awaken their interests for learning and reading. Strict and frightening attitudes and words are to be avoided. Islamic values may be analyzed with comparison to that of other systems'. The general condition of the world, worldwide problems of Muslims and their possible solutions could be elaborated upon.

At the festival of *Eid al-Fitr*, cultural and human dimensions may be told of, whereas, at *Eid al-Adha* economic and social statuses should be addressed. However, they can also be discussed alongside principles of faith, unity and elements of morality.

## Blessed Nights

Auspicious blessed nights, though they are not as common as festivals are, have a great impact on society and are one of the happiest reasons for coming to mosques. Since long ago, these nights were celebrated with different names. Only at the period of the Ottoman Sultan Selim II's reign (1566–1574), on the occasion of these nights mosques were brightened with torchlights that were put on minarets, did these nights become known as *Kandil* (torchlight) Nights. These nights are *Mawlid* (blessed night of the noble birth of the Prophet), *Laylatul Raghaib* (the Night of Hopes; *Raghaib* is celebrated on the night preceding the first Friday of the month Rajab), *Laylatul Miraj* (the Night of the Ascension), *Laylatul Barat* (the Night of Salvation) and *Laylatul Qadr* (the Night of Destiny and Power). According to lunar calendar, the dates of these nights are: *Laylatul Mawlid* is on the twelfth night of the month of Rabi al-awwal (the third month of Islamic calendar), *Laylatul Raghaib* is on the first Friday of the month of Rajab (the seventh month of the Islamic calendar), *Laylatul Miraj* is on the twenty seventh day of the same month, *Laylatul Barat* in on the fifteenth night of the month of Shaban (the eighth month of the Islamic calendar) and *Laylatul Qadr* (the Night of Destiny and Power) is on the twenty seventh night of the month of Ramadan (the ninth month of the Islamic calendar).

### *Laylatul Mawlid*

The word *Mawlid* means time and place of birth. Colloquially, this a term is used in a broad meaning that encompasses our Prophet's honoring this world, different kinds of practices done on the occasion of this day, and eulogies and poems about the noble Messenger of Allah. An actual point of reciting and letting others recite eulogies is to reveal joy for the Prophet's favoring this world, to put into word one's love and longing for him, and to remember some events of his noble life. On the occasion of that day, people gather at some place within the rightful circle to deliver religious discourses, invoke peace and blessings to the Prophet, offer treats, present gifts, consolidate kinship and community consciousness, and sing certain eulogies praising our Prophet. As a matter of fact, the Presidency of Religious Affairs does successfully perform religious activities during the Week of Blessed Birth by approaching them from different points of view. It is really a great activity to tell to people about the Prophet in such a way.

Though there exist different kinds of implementations, in short, the ceremonies of Blessed Night of *Mawlid* take place in the following way:

A foundation or a person organizes a ceremony for the night of the Prophet's birth.

People who gather for this ceremony listen to a person, preferably with a good voice, who recites verses from the Holy Qur'an, religious chants and eulogies, invokes peace and blessings to Prophet, and makes supplications; another person, who has knowledge concerning religious matters, gives a speech (on religion), after which prepared food is eaten. Rewards of all those deeds are bestowed to antecedents of the organizers of the ceremony. A eulogy about the noble Messenger of Allah, written by Süleyman Çelebi *Wasilat'un Najat* is a popularly recited piece at these ceremonies.

Moreover, there are eulogies recited besides the ones uttered on the Night of Blessed Birth. Commonly, eulogies are recited on the occasion of turning back from pilgrimage, at weddings or circumcisions, when recovering from an illness, when beginning a new business or at other events of joy, or, when someone dies or gets martyred. At eulogies recited for happy events, thanking Allah for bestowing favors and possibilities is the focus. As for a purpose of reciting eulogies for the dead, then it is done for devoting rewards to the dead's soul.

Concerning eulogies, these elements should be paid attention to:
a. Texts of eulogies should never be considered as sacred as a text of the Holy Qur'an. Nor are they as revered as texts of the noble *hadiths*.

b. Many believe that a person reading a eulogy commercializes the act by bargaining for a great amount of money. Such a commercial concept will spoil the purity of a reward-oriented act and deserves (nothing other than) criticism. It should not be welcomed by anyone. However, by being inspired by our Prophet's presenting his own gown, there is no objection in presenting a gift to the person reciting the eulogy, assuming you are obeying the Prophet and there is no bargaining.

c. When everything is done for the sake of earning rewards (from Allah,) and one is speaking about our Prophet, everyone, especially reciters, is expected to be serious and sincere. Ceremonies where people do not behave and dress up inappropriately or where a feeling of compassion is not present, will be misguided and pave the way for criticism. Will any rewards be obtained? That is a matter for discussion. An Assembly of *Mawlid*, a place of respect and sincerity, must be an environment of entreaty and supplication, an opportunity for spiritual nourishment and ascension.

d. Because some eulogies are delivered differently, in strange accents, it is possible that sometimes they will not bring forth heartfelt tremors, deluges of feelings, and self-orderliness among listeners. Such an implementation, in fact, may mostly result in loss rather than benefit. Yet, there is no room for indolence, heedlessness, showing off and a conception of "for form's sake," where lofty truths are spoken of.

e. People with sound finances using their wealth in extravagant fashion, such as handing out disbursements or treats to indulge the audience or those reciting the eulogy, are not welcome. Such actions take away from the purity of the event.

### Laylatul Qadr

The word "*qadr*" means "rule, honor, power and loftiness". In the chapter of Al-Qadr, the night when the Holy Qur'an was revealed, is called as *Laylatul Qadr*. Revealing the Holy Qur'an, which is the last address and final message from Allah the Almighty to His Messenger marks a turning point in humanity's road to truth. The night when revelation took place bears a significant meaning. In the *hadith*, which points to the significance of *Laylatul Qadr*, it is stated that in response to the preceding community's long lives and their chances to earn rewards due to that, Muslims were granted with the Night of Destiny and Power.[12]

> The angels and the Spirit descend in it by the permission of their Lord with His decrees for every affair. (Being) a sheer mercy and security (from all misfortunes, for the servants who spend it in devotions in appreciation of its worth), (being) until the rising of the dawn. (al-Qadr 97:4-5)

This *hadith* gives us glad tidings of being forgiven all the previous sins of those who revived *Laylatul Qadr* by believing in it and expecting rewards for it from the Allah the Almighty.[13] On the last ten days of the month of Ramadan, our beloved Prophet used to seclude himself in the mosque by drawing away from worldly things, spending his nights worshiping and contemplating. He used to encourage his family to do the same, too.[14] The noble Messenger of Allah advised us to make the following supplication at the Night of Qadr:

اللَّهُمَّ إِنَّكَ عَفُوٌّ تُحِبُّ الْعَفْوَ فَاعْفُ عَنِّي

*"O Allah! You are a forgiver and love forgiving! Do forgive my sins, too."*[15]

Therefore, Muslims make efforts to spend the last night of Ramadan, and especially, the twenty seventh night of it, worshiping, conscious of servitude, and decide not to repeat their past mistakes. As the word "*qadr*" means dignity, value and merit, it has to do with Divine power, too. It is like Allah's treating us with His Divine power more than with His wisdom in the Hereafter. In the same way, at that Night of Destiny and Power, His power is prevailing more than His wisdom. For those, who know the value of that night, Allah will grant His favors abundantly. In other words, Mus-

---

[12] *Muwatta*, Itiqaf, 6
[13] *Sahih al-Bukhari*, Fazlu Laylatul Qadr, 1
[14] *Sahih al-Bukhari*, Fazlu Laylatul Qadr, 5
[15] *Sunan at-Tirmidhi*, Dawat, 84

lims will be given rewards in the Hereafter. At *Laylatul Qadr* an appreciative spirit encompasses everything.

This night is more favorable than thousands of months are. It is a period of time, which delivers many kinds of benevolences. Those who comprehend and respect this night in an appropriate way may earn benevolence. As a matter of fact, within a single moment of Friday, the hour of acceptance, there is nestled a condensed pellet of opportunities. A few minutes encompass several years. For instance, the Ascension of the Prophet (the miraculous journeying of the Prophet Muhammad, peace and blessings be upon him, through the realms of existence, beyond the limit of forms, during which he witnessed the supreme signs of Allah) took place in the same manner. Just a short time of Ascension had covered thousands of years.

The exact night of *Laylatul Qadr* is not defined. A maxim of "Do consider each night as Qadr and each person as Khidr[16]" is short but very inclusive. Khidr has a personality, which is hidden among people, so that no one can know who he is. However, if you are respectful of everyone, and help everyone who is needy, then one day you will come across Khidr, a person of belief, and the gardens of your heart will blossom. As *Laylatul Qadr* in Ramadan, eminent friends of Allah among people, the hour of acceptance on Fridays, the Greatest Name (the most universal name of Allah) among the All-Beautiful Names of Allah (these Names are either included in the Holy Qur'an or were taught by Allah's Messenger, and Allah is and should be called by them) and the appointed hour of death in life remain unknown, then all the rest, i.e. all Muslims, hours of Fridays, names of Allah the Almighty and all nights of Ramadan must be dear to us and taken very seriously. If they were definite, then others could have lost their meaning.

The importance of *Laylatul Qadr* in the Holy Qur'an and in the *hadiths* is in the acceptance by Allah of all acts of worship and supplications performed that night. Statements of our noble Prophet on the evanescence of the sins of those who do revive this night became a motivation for Muslim communities

---

[16] Khidr is a spiritual personality and a man of wisdom in Islamic tradition, who lives in an angelic way, serving Allah in the execution of His commands and succoring people in hard conditions.

to pay much attention to *Laylatul Qadr*. This has been reflected in an enrichment of customs and traditions. Previous Islamic communities have constituted a rich tradition of special kinds of religious practices and supplications for *Laylatul Qadr*, and endowments involving relevant formalities and ceremonies. It is common practice, on the Night of Qadr, to make a prayer out of finishing the recitation of the whole Qur'an that was started at the beginning of Ramadan. It became a custom to receive supplications from a *hafiz* (a person who has completely memorized the Qur'an) and respectable reciters of prayers at different mosques. It is known that at large mosques, supplications of these kinds were uttered till Morning Prayers. Moreover, sermons were given at mosques and Dervish lodges, where, besides common people, religious scholars, saints and prominent statesmen used to take part.

## Laylatul Barat

The word "*barat*" means forgiving sins of sinners.

In the following verse there is an allusion for the *Laylatul Barat*: "*We sent it down on a night full of blessings; surely We have ever been warning (humankind since their creation)*" (ad-Dukhan 44:3).

According to some interpreters of the Holy Qur'an, that night is the Night of Qadr and according to others—it is the Night of Barat. It is narrated that our Prophet used to perform religious practices at the very night and fast during the daytime of that night. The famous interpreter of the Holy Qur'an, Muhammad Hamdi Yazır from Elmalı, in the commentary of the verse gave the following information on the grounds of noble *hadith*s: There are five traits of that night.

1. Every deed that bears paramount importance and Divine wisdom will be managed and distributed. They will be particularly separated so as to be fulfilled.
2. It is very virtuous to worship that night. The Messenger of Allah stated: "If someone performs a Prayer of one hundred units that night, then Allah will send to him one hundred angels. Thirty of them will give him glad tidings of Paradise, another thirty will assure him of being saved from Hellfire, and another thirty will ward off worldly

catastrophes from him. As for the remaining ten, then they will wean the traps and guiles of Satan."

3. Almighty Allah will send His mercy. The Prophet decreed the following: "That night Allah will bestow His mercy on people more than the number of the hair of the sheep of Banu Kalb."
4. Allah will grant forgiveness that night. Once again, our Messenger said: "That night Allah will forgive all Muslims, except soothsayers, sorcerers, malevolent ones, alcoholics, those who hurt their parents and continue committing adultery."
5. That night the right of intercession was given completely to the Messenger of Allah. On the thirteenth night of the month of Shaban, the Messenger of Allah supplicated for the intercession of his community. That time only one-third of his wish was granted to him. On the fourteenth night he again supplicated for attaining intercession. This time two-thirds of his wish was given to him. On the fifteenth night he supplicated again; this time the entire wish was given to him. However, it was not the case for those, who flee from Allah the Almighty, as camels do.[17]

From the narration of the noble Messenger of Allah regarding the virtues of the month of Rajab, it becomes quite clear that he had especially cherished it. By passage of time, Muslims lionized the first Friday nights of three blessed months and started to revive them. Referring to a noble *hadith*, they named it as *Raghaib*. One more blessed night of the month of Rajab is the Night of Ascension. On that night, praying five times became an obligatory religious duty for all Muslims. Moreover, glad tidings of Muslims being forgiven, unless they associate partners to Allah, were given to our Prophet. When this *hadith* was studied together with narrations concerning intercession, this night became a Blessed Night that is worthy of celebrating.

Though our people do not have splendor and wealth as they used to have, they do pay a lot of attention to religious festivals in comparison to other days. For instance, the following things are done at festivals:

---

[17] Yazır, *Hak Dini Kur'an Dili*, 8:5869

- people gather at neighbor's houses to prepare pastry rings and halva (a sweet prepared with sesame oil, various cereals, and syrup or honey);
- minarets are decorated with dangling lights that spell out devotional messages in huge letters, suspended between the minarets;
- people fast during the daytimes of festivals;
- friends congratulate one another;
- eulogies are recited;
- people worship a lot and give alms;
- special meetings are organized in mosques;
- sermons are delivered;

Many people take part at these activities, even those who have never gone to Friday Prayers. Therefore, it is important for the day's preachers to be well prepared. There is historic information concerning the subject, particular characteristics, related verses and *hadith*s of each festival. Taking those into consideration, we can give basic headings or a plan of sermons:

a. Importance of the Blessed Night in religion and its position in history;
b. Causes that made the night special;
c. Influence of the night to Muslims beliefs and deeds;
d. Favors of the night;
e. Religious practices and duties to be done that night;
f. Congratulating one another and uttering supplications.

## ASSESSMENT

1. How many festivals are there in Islam?
2. What is the difference between the Blessed Nights and festivals?
3. Write three verses of the Holy Qur'an concerning the Blessed Nights.
4. Write three *hadith*s concerning festivals.
5. What does "*Laylatul Qadr*'s being more auspicious than a thousand months" mean?

# UNIT 4

## BEING AN IMAM AND MUEZZIN

# BEING AN IMAM AND MUEZZIN

## Definition of Imam and Muezzin, and Their Importance and Position in History

"Imam" literally means "to be ahead of, to motivate and to supervise;" as a term, it means "a leader of a congregational Prayer, to whom others do obey."

Being an imam is an important duty that started as soon as the five Daily Prayers became obligatory for Muslims. Archangel Gabriel taught our Prophet how to lead a Prayer. First, our Prophet started to lead Prayers by Holy Ka'ba and, later, due to the oppression of the polytheists, at some houses in isolated parts of Mecca, with those who obeyed him[18]. A command that took place in the 110th verse of the chapter of Al-Isra, *"And offer your Prayer neither in too loud a voice nor in a voice too low, but follow a middle course,"* was given so that the polytheists would not be aware of Prayers[19]. Right after the first Aqaba Pledge, Mus'ab ibn Umayr and As'ad ibn Zurara were sent to Medina, where they started to lead the Daily Prayers and Friday Prayers regularly. Before the *Hijra* (migration), imam of the Quba Muslims was the freed slave of Abu Huzayfa, Salim. He was known as imam of migrants. During the time of migration, before entering

---

[18] *Musnad*, I, 333
[19] *Musnad*, I, 23

the territory of Medina, our Prophet built a mosque in Quba. Salim was the imam of that mosque.

When the noble Messenger of Allah parted from Medina, he would appoint an imam by proxy. When his illness worsened and he could not move from his wife Aisha's room to the Masjid an-Nabawi, he appointed Abu Bakr as imam. When the Prophet appointed imams to districts and tribes who were newly converted to Islam, he used to pay attention to their knowledge of the Holy Qur'an, especially their ability of reciting and comprehending it.

This practice of our Prophet, and his admonitions, increased the importance of mosques. Throughout history, mosques were centers where people used to gather, pray, obtain knowledge and improve their spirit of unity. Imams were spiritual mentors that united and guided this community.

Being an imam, which is a very important and virtuous duty, is also a serious responsibility.

The importance of an imam's duties is obviously seen in the religious sources. A person who deserves a position of imam must obtain knowledge of *Sunnah* and Islamic Jurisprudence in the best way. If there are candidates with equal knowledge of *Sunnah*, then the one who recites the Qur'an in the best way must be chosen as imam. If they recite the Holy Qur'an equally well, then priority should be given to the most pious of them. If they are equal in all those three qualities, then the elder one should be chosen. If their ages are equal, then the one, who has better manners (who has a soft temperament and is the most modest one) should be chosen. If they are equal in this quality, too, then preference should be given to those who are the most handsome, come from the most honorable tribe, possess the most beautiful voice and wear the cleanest outfits. In case they are equal in those last qualities, too, then lots should be drawn by them. Nevertheless, if there is a host of the house or an appointed imam of that place, then he should be preferred for a position of imam, even though they do not have all of those above mentioned qualities.

If so then, the most important element of a person assigned for that duty should be his connection with Allah, his sincerity and purity of intentions, and his being an exemplary individual concerning his religious practices and morals. Imams, who practice their preaching, are spiritual leaders and counselors of their community. Therefore, they should improve themselves and continuously involve with learning and teaching activities. They should be sincere and friendly with the community, and have good communications with their addressees. Issues that imams should pay attention to are taking care of his own appearance, being perceptive to problems around him and finding solution to them, trying his best to be a good preacher, reciting the Holy Qur'an according to *tajwid* rules (rules governing pronunciation during recitations of the Qur'an) with an expressive voice, supervising his district's people and ensuring they are not in contradiction with Islamic values. These points are valid for muezzins, too.

"Muezzin" means the one who invites and recites *adhan* and *iqamah*. In the first periods of Islam, Bilal al-Habashi used to call for Prayers on the streets of Medina with the words of "*As-salah, as-salah* (It's time to pray)", such an implementation was not considered to be enough. On the first (622) and second (623) years after the Hijra, the Messenger of Allah defined the wordings of *adhan*, with which the codes of muezzins emerged. After that date, those who invited to Prayer and recited *iqamah* were called as muezzins.

It was Bilal al-Habashi, who recited *adhan* on the roof of the house of a woman from the Najjar tribe. The Messenger of Allah wanted governors and tribes, newly converted to Islam, to appoint someone among them for a position of imam and muezzin.

Since the Age of Happiness, imams and muezzins were selected among those who had a beautiful and stentorian voice, recited the Holy Qur'an in the best way, and were aware of music. It is narrated that the Messenger of Allah listened to twenty reciters of *adhan* and then only liked Abu Mahzura's voice among them and taught the words of *adhan* to him[20]. Abu Mahzura, who fulfilled his duty in the Ka'ba and taught *adhan* recitation his whole long life, was a founder of the Meccan recitation of *adhan*; Sad ibn

---

[20] *Darimi*, Salah, 7

Aidh was founder of the Medinan recitation. At regions, where Islam was spread, muezzins used to base their *adhans* on either way.

A tradition of offering glorifications from minarets on special days and, particularly, before the Night and Morning Prayers, as well as on Fridays and at the Blessed Nights, and reciting peace and blessings to our Prophet before Friday Prayers, was carried out for the first time in the mosque of Amr ibn As in Egypt during the governance of Maslama ibn Muhallad (d. 682). Later on, this practice, with Qur'an recitation, supplications, chants and eulogies, was spread throughout the entire Islamic word.[21]

In the past, significant number of muezzins used to be interested in not just music, but other branches of fine art. They used to perform many kinds of mosque music, including the recitation of glorifications, supplications, litanies, calling for Prayer, *takbir* (Allahu Akbar), eulogies recited to celebrate the Blessed Birth of Prophet Muhammad, peace and blessings be upon him, topics on the Ascension, and chants. Moreover, besides calling to Prayer, death announcements were made from minarets and two kinds of prayers were uttered: during funeral ceremonies (the act of taking a corpse to the grave) and after the burial. At palaces and some other mansions, famous muezzins used to gather for *Tarawih* (a *sunnah* Prayer peculiar to Ramadan, observed at night). Chants that others recited here with those muezzins were called as "Ramadan Chants."

Being a muezzin is considered to be one of the most virtuous of righteous deeds. Prophet Muhammad, peace and blessings be upon him, emphasized the significance of being muezzin and said:

"If people were aware of rewards given for muezzins and those who stand on first line of congregational Prayers, they would draw lots to attain these positions."[22]

---

[21] *Maqrizi*, IX, 51
[22] *Sahih al-Bukhari*, Adhan, 8

"If someone does recite *adhan* for seven years by awaiting reward for it, then Allah the Almighty will make a muniment for his salvation from Hellfire."[23]

"At the Day of Resurrection, muezzins would be the tallest among other people."[24]

The following qualities and actions are recommended for muezzins:
- a stentorian and beautiful voice;
- reciting *adhan* in standing position and with pauses in between so that listeners have a chance to repeat after him;
- putting the tips of his index fingers against the lobes of his ears or putting his hands against his ears in order to help his voice come out clearly;
- facing the *qiblah* (the direction in which a Muslim turns to when praying);
- turning to the right while saying *Hayya ala's-salah* (Come to pray), turning to the left while saying *Hayya ala'l-falah* (Come to salvation);
- pronouncing the words *As-salatu khayrun min'an-nawm* (Prayer is better than sleep) twice after *Hayya ala'l-falah* for the Morning Prayer;
- being on different parts of the minaret balcony while reciting *adhan*;
- performing *wudu* (minor ablution) before reciting *adhan*

## Paying Wages to Imams and Muezzins

Obeying Allah's commands and avoiding His prohibitions, while performing religious practices, are acts of submission to Allah. In the same way, reciting the Holy Qur'an, teaching it, being an imam or muezzin, being a *mufti* (the religious authority officially charged in towns to explain religious matters and direct religious affairs), and preaching are acts of submission to Allah. Hence, it is conflictual for them to take wages for their work. Those who had negative views concerning this matter, alongside the *hadiths* and the words of the Companions, which recommended not taking money for

---

[23] *Sunan at-Tirmidhi*, Salah, 152
[24] *Sahih Muslim*, Salah, 14

being an imam or muezzin (*Ibn Majah*, Adhan, 3; *Sunan Abu Dawud*, Salah, 40), rationally propounded such facts that worship would be accepted only if it is done for Allah's sake and that accomplishing religious practices for some amount of money would not be accepted as a desired act. In early times, scholars of Hanafi and Hanbali schools had a policy of not receiving money for reciting *adhan*; i.e. it was not a permissible act for them. As for the scholars of Shafi and Maliki schools, the latter was a permissible act. Lately, with a decrease in the volunteers to be muezzins, Hanafi school gave permission for them paying wages. However, it is perfectly acceptable to not take wages to fulfill the duty of imam, and to complimentarily teach the Holy Qur'an, *hadiths*, and other religious studies. For, telling about religion and teaching its commands to others is a duty of the Prophets. And taking wages for such acts was not a matter in question for the Prophets. Some of the characteristics of the path of Prophethood are endeavor, resolution, devotion, and contentedness. They have dignified contentment towards everyone but Allah.[25]

However, if a person does not have any other possibility of providing a living for his family, or if there is even a slight risk of his dealing with forbidden or doubtful things as a means of making his living, then he must get some amount of money, even though he does service of religion. There must be no objection to that.

## Duties of Imam and Muezzin

Nowadays, the basic duty of an imam is to lead Prayers and deliver sermons, whereas a muezzin's duties are to recite *adhan*, *iqamah*, and the Beautiful Names of Allah and to send blessings to the noble Prophet (after each obligatory Prayer). Certainly, besides these basic tasks and official duties there are other duties, which were formed due to customs and traditions and which may vary depending on location. For example, in the circular note of the Presidency of Religious Affairs of Turkey, the following points are known to be duties of imams and muezzins:

---

[25] See, Yunus 10:72; Ash-Shu'ara 26:109, 127, 145, 164, 180.

## Duties of Imam and the Preacher

a. alongside the five Daily Prayers, leading Friday, *Eid, Tarawih* and Funeral Prayers;
b. delivering Friday and *Eid* sermons on time and meticulously;
c. teaching the religious subjects to the community, according to subjects given to them by religious authority;
d. teaching the Holy Qur'an at mosques or other appropriate places, by the permission of the local administrator of religious affairs, to those who want to learn, and providing them with knowledge of religion, including accomplishing their duties concerning summer Qur'an courses;
e. taking necessary measures at mosques, where lessons are given;
f. reciting the Holy Qur'an, depending on necessity, before or after the five Daily Prayers;
g. reciting the Qur'anic verses and fulfilling the duties in the meetings organized by religious authorities on the Blessed Nights and Days;
h. performing a religious ceremony of marriage after the marriage contract made according to Civil Code;
i. keeping the mosques and its surrounding clean; outsourcing cleaning service for the fountain (reservoir with faucets at the sides for ablutions) and restrooms;
j. providing funeral services if there is no municipal organization;
k. fulfilling the duties of muezzins in their absence.

## Duties of Muezzins

a. To open and close mosques at times determined by the local administrator of religious affairs;
b. To recite *adhan* for the five Daily Prayers according to a timetable;
c. To accomplish different kinds of muezzin services, required by religious rituals, during the five Daily Prayers, *Eid, Tarawih* and Funeral Prayers, and to say *takbir* and *salah*, if required;

d. To assist the imam in teaching the Holy Qur'an and religious subjects to people;
e. To read Qur'anic verses and fulfill the duties in the meetings organized by religious authorities on the Blessed Nights and Days;
f. To fulfill the duties of imams in their absence.

### The Terms and Regulations of *Adhan*

The following are instructions for the recitation of *adhan* and *iqamah*:

1. *Adhan* consists of these sacred words:

$$
\text{اللهُ اَكْبَرُ اللهُ اَكْبَرُ — اللهُ اَكْبَرُ اللهُ اَكْبَرُ}
$$

$$
\text{اَشْهَدُ اَنْ لَا اِلٰهَ اِلَّا اللهُ — اَشْهَدُ اَنْ لَا اِلٰهَ اِلَّا اللهُ}
$$

$$
\text{اَشْهَدُ اَنَّ مُحَمَّدًا رَسُولُ اللهِ — اَشْهَدُ اَنَّ مُحَمَّدًا رَسُولُ اللهِ}
$$

$$
\text{حَىَّ عَلَى الصَّلَاةِ — حَىَّ عَلَى الصَّلَاةِ}
$$

$$
\text{حَىَّ عَلَى الْفَلَاحِ — حَىَّ عَلَى الْفَلَاحِ}
$$

$$
\text{اللهُ اَكْبَرُ اللهُ اَكْبَرُ}
$$

$$
\text{لَا اِلٰهَ اِلَّا اللهُ}
$$

*Allahu akbar* (Allah is the All-Great) (four times)
*Ash-hadu an-la ilaha illa'llah* (I bear witness that there is no deity but Allah) (twice)
*Ash-hadu anna Muhammad'ar-Rasulullah* (I bear witness that Muhammad is the Messenger of Allah) (twice)
*Hayya ala's-salah* (Come to the Prayer) (twice)
*Hayya ala'l-falah* (Come to salvation) (twice)
*Allahu akbar* (Allah is the All-Great) (twice)
*La ilaha illa'llah* (There is no deity but Allah) (once)

الصلوة خير من النوم *As-salatu khayrun min'an-nawm* (Prayer is better than sleep) is recited only during the *adhan* of the Morning Prayer twice, and قَدْ قَامَتِ الصَّلَاة *Qad qamat'us-salah* (Now, the Prayer is about to begin) is recited only during the *iqamah* twice, after *Hayya ala'l-falah* both.

2. There is a pause between each sentence of *adhan*. Each following sentence is recited with an increased voice. It is called as *tarassul* (at an easy pace). The words of *iqamah* are recited ceaselessly. *Adhan* and *iqamah* should be recited in Arabic, and with an appropriate tune. The translations cannot be equivalent of the original texts of *adhan* and *iqamah*, which are the prominent signs of Islam.
3. One *adhan* and one *iqamah* is recited for each of the five Daily Prayers. Exclusively, there are two *adhans* recited on Friday Prayers. No *iqamah* is recited for *Witr, Eid* Prayers, *Tarawih* and other supererogatory Prayers;
4. It is very virtuous to recite *adhan* and *iqamah* for Prayers performed at home or outside. One can recite only *iqamah*, but reciting only *adhan* is discouraged;
5. It is appropriate to have some pause between *adhan* and *iqamah*;
6. *Adhan* and *iqamah* are *sunnah* acts of five Daily Prayers as well as they are the one for the *Qada* (Compensatory) Prayers;
7. If such acts like eating, drinking and washing are done in between *adhan* and *iqamah*, then the *iqamah* should be recited again;
8. It is approved for muezzins to know *Sunnah* of the Prophet and to be pious; it is discouraged for ignorant and evildoers to recite *adhan*;
9. It is recommended to recite the *adhan,* which was called by a drunk, an insane person or a child who did not reach the age of puberty, again. According to some scholars it is necessary to recite it again;
10. It is discouraged to recite *adhan* in a sitting position;
11. It is discouraged to make *talhin* (quavering voice) while reciting *adhan*;
12. While reciting *adhan* and *iqamah*, muezzin should be in a standing position with his face turned towards the *qiblah*. He should turn to the right when saying *"Hayya alas-salah"* and to the left when say-

ing "Hayya alal-falah". If he is on a minaret, then he should recite by going to the right and then to the left;

13. Talking between *adhan* and *iqamah* is discouraged;
14. People must listen to *adhan*, while it is being recited;
15. While listening to *adhan* and *iqamah*, it is recommended to repeat it word for word. However, when muezzin recites *Hayya alas-salah; Hayya alal-falah*, one should say: لَا حَوْلَ وَ لَا قُوَّةَ اِلَّا بِالله *La hawla wa la kuwwata illa billah* (There is neither strength nor power save with Allah). In the *adhan* of the Morning Prayer, when muezzin says اَلصَّلَاةُ خَيْرٌ مِنْ النَّوْمِ *As-salatu khayrun min'an-nawm* (Prayer is better than sleep) one should say: *Sadaqta wa bararta* (You have spoken the truth and done a good deed).
16. A Muslim, who listens to *adhan* must recite the following supplication:

$$\text{للّٰهُمَّ رَبَّ هٰذِهِ الدَّعْوَةِ التَّامَّةِ وَالصَّلَاةِ الْقَائِمَةِ اٰتِ سَيِّدَنَا}$$

$$\text{مُحَمَّدًا الْوَسِيلَةَ وَالْفَضِيلَةَ وَالدَّرَجَةَ الرَّفِيعَةَ وَابْعَثْهُ مَقَامًا}$$

$$\text{مَحْمُودًا الَّذِي وَعَدْتَهُ إِنَّكَ لَا تُخْلِفُ الْمِيعَادَ}$$

(O Allah! Lord of this call [to Prayer] that has been completed, and the ritual prayer that is about to be performed, grant our master Muhammad nearness to You, reaching Paradise and beyond, and exalt him to the praised station of intercession that You promised him. You do not do anything against Your promise).

## ASSESSMENT

1. Should imams get wages for their work?
2. Write down the duties of muezzins.
3. What kinds of characteristics should an appropriate *adhan* have?
4. Write down the supplications of *adhan*.
5. What characteristics should imams have?

# UNIT 5

## RELIGIOUS ORATORY AND SUPPLICATION

# RELIGIOUS ORATORY AND SUPPLICATION

## Supplication

Religion, in a broad sense of it, is a position and attitude of creatures towards the Creator. The Holy Qur'an gives the following names to that attitude—glorification, praise and prostration.[26] The given above are considered as kinds of supplication, which itself is a generic concept. Even the word of *salah*, which is mentioned in the Holy Qur'an and *hadith*s as the religious practice of the five Daily Prayers, means "supplication." Concepts of sanctification, prostration, exaltation and gratefulness bear approximately the same meaning. As a matter of fact, our Prophet says, "The essence of worship is supplication."[27] In other words, the essence of all religious practices lies in supplication.

Supplication does not only mean asking the things we need. It is realizing our absolute helplessness and poverty before Allah the Almighty, Who creates and gives life to us. It is the awareness of the fact that we are not self-sufficient. It is expounding our inner world in the presence of our Lord, Who knows and understands us best of all, and sincerely confessing our states to Him. It is being in private with a Real Friend and True Beloved. Therefore, a

---
[26] Ar-Ra'd 13:13, al-Isra 17:44, an-Nur 24:41
[27] *Sunan at-Tirmidhi*, Dawat, 1

supplication is, first of all, getting rid of evil feelings and thoughts, and attaining tranquility of the soul by means of being imbued with good feelings.

Supplication is not sounds and words, uttered from our mouths, but it is yearning of hearts and the longing of souls. In the Holy Qur'an that point is emphasized as follows:

> Call upon your Lord (O humankind) with humility and in the secrecy of your hearts. Indeed your Lord does not love those who exceed the bounds. (Keep within the bounds He has decreed). Do not cause disorder and corruption on the earth seeing that it has been so well ordered, and call upon Him with fear (of His punishment) and longing (for His forgiveness and mercy). Allah's mercy is indeed near to those devoted to doing good, aware that Allah is seeing them. (al-A'raf 7:55–56)

Supplication is a measure of a person's value:

"Say: 'My Lord would not care for you were it not for your Prayer'" (al-Furqan 25:77).

In fact, supplication is a very important part of this life and the Hereafter. Nowadays, it is minimized and used-up after just the five Daily Prayers and after some other practices. It is impossible to think about this life without the presence of supplications. Actually, life consists entirely of supplications. It is a key to the pleasure of Allah and the abode of Paradise. It is, also, a sign of servitude and Allah's mercy[28]. Rather, it is a focal point of the relation between a servant and the Almighty. Supplication is a Divine ascension that connects the world of contingencies with the realm of the Transcendental Manifestation of Divinity. Therefore, the most acceptable supplication is the believer's ascension, which is uttered at the time of prostration.[29]

Descent of Divine mercy happens due to our supplications. Supplication functions like a lightning arrester against wrath. In other words, supplication is an effective act of worship that invokes Divine mercy and pleasure, while concurrently dispelling Divine wrath from us. Whenever a person has no other possibilities left, he starts to supplicate sincerely. In fact, it

---

[28] Daylami, *Al-Firdaws*, II, 224
[29] *Sahih Muslim*, Salah, 215

is impossible to determine its starting and ending points. For, there is no single moment when a person will feel himself contented with his supplications. In that case, a person should not be away from supplications just like our Lord is not away from us, even for a moment, with His manifestations.

From the point of view of a person, supplication is asking for some things. However, most people do not know the way of asking, and misbehave. To be more explicit, a person would like to see the absolute Divine Will dependent on his free will. Unquestionably, a supplication made with such an attitude and intention will never be a true supplication, which is a deep and sincere connection between a person and the Almighty, glorified and exalted be He. For, being well-mannered and humble while uttering a supplication is a first condition of its acceptance. Therefore, a person, while presenting his thoughts and feelings to Allah, should struggle to express it in the best way. He should strive to use fewer, more meaningful words. The biggest help here, as in any other matter, is from the Holy Qur'an and *Hadith* books. For, Allah, Who gives us the ability to ask questions, teaches us the ways of asking them, too. Surely a person, to whom the most beautiful and effective supplications were taught, is the Messenger of Allah. His blessed life was full of supplications. Considering the collection of his supplications, it becomes clear that he was a unique individual. It is as if our noble Prophet spent each and every moment of his life supplicating. It would be wise to observe his way of uttering supplications.

If we look at daily supplications of our Prophet, then the following brief classifications may be made:

1. Supplications uttered at certain times of the day;
2. Supplications made because of good or bad events;
3. Supplications uttered during, before and after having food, sleeping, worry and glory, dressing, entering a mosque, home or restrooms, and leaving such places;
4. Supplications made while having an ablution;
5. Supplications made in and after the Prayers;
6. Repentances and asking for forgiveness.

Below, we have tried to give you supplications that a preacher makes during accomplishing his duties, supplications that can be uttered at different moments of life, and other necessary supplications. The major part of these supplications was done by the Messenger of Allah and the remaining part was done by later, pious scholars on the grounds of the *Sunnah*, and practices and words of the Companions of the Prophet.

Supplications of Sermons

At the first step of the pulpit:

اِفْتَحْ عَلَيْنَا اَبْوَابَ رَحْمَتِكَ وَيَسِّرْ عَلَيْنَا خَزَائِنَ فَضْلِكَ وَكَرَمِكَ يَا اَكْرَمَ الْاَكْرَمِينَ وَيَا اَرْحَمَ الرَّاحِمِينَ اَللّٰهُمَّ

(O Allah! Open for us the gates of Your mercy, open up for us the treasures of Your Mercy. You are the most Generous of the Generous! You are the most Merciful of the Merciful!)

At the third step:

رَبِّ اشْرَحْ لِي صَدْرِي وَيَسِّرْ لِي أَمْرِي وَاحْلُلْ عُقْدَةً مِنْ لِسَانِي يَفْقَهُوا قَوْلِي ۞ رَبِّ قَدْ اٰتَيْتَنِي مِنَ الْمُلْكِ وَعَلَّمْتَنِي مِنْ تَأْوِيلِ الْاَحَادِيثِ ۞ رَبِّ زِدْنِي عِلْمًا وَفَهْمًا وَاَلْحِقْنِي بِالصَّالِحِينَ

(My Lord, expand for me my breast. Make my task easy for me. Loosen a knot from my tongue (to make my speech more fluent) so that they may understand my speech clearly. My Lord! You have indeed granted me some important part of the rule and imparted to me some knowledge of the inner meaning of all happenings (including dreams). O You, Originator of the heavens and the earth, each with particular features! You are my Owner and Guardian in this world and in the Hereafter. Take my soul to You as a Muslim, and join me with the righteous).

At the fifth or seventh step:

$$
\text{اَللّٰهُمَّ هٰذَا الشَّانُ لَيْسَ بِشَانِي وَهٰذَا الْمَكَانُ لَيْسَ بِمَكَانِي ۝ اَللّٰهُمَّ يَسِّرْ لِي اَمْرِي وَتَقَبَّلْهُ مِنِّي ۝ وَسَلَامٌ عَلٰى جَمِيعِ الْاَنْبِيَاءِ وَالْمُرْسَلِينَ ۝ وَالْحَمْدُ لِلّٰهِ رَبِّ الْعَالَمِينَ
$$

(O my Lord, this state is not mine, neither is this position mine! Do facilitate my duty and accept it! Greetings to all Your Prophets and Messengers! All Praises belong to You, the Lord of the Universe!)

Supplication uttered during the first sermon:

$$
\text{اَلْحَمْدُ لِلّٰهِ نَحْمَدُهُ وَنَسْتَعِينُهُ وَنَسْتَغْفِرُهُ وَنَعُوذُ بِاللّٰهِ مِنْ شُرُورِ اَنْفُسِنَا وَمِنْ سَيِّئَاتِ اَعْمَالِنَا ۝ مَنْ يَهْدِ اللّٰهُ فَلَا مُضِلَّ لَهُ وَمَنْ يُضْلِلْ فَلَا هَادِيَ لَهُ ۝ نَشْهَدُ اَنْ لَا اِلٰهَ اِلَّا اللّٰهُ وَحْدَهُ لَا شَرِيكَ لَهُ وَنَشْهَدُ اَنَّ سَيِّدَنَا مُحَمَّدًا عَبْدُهُ وَرَسُولُهُ ۝ اَللّٰهُمَّ صَلِّ وَسَلِّمْ عَلٰى سَيِّدِنَا مُحَمَّدٍ وَعَلٰى اٰلِهِ وَاَصْحَابِهِ اَجْمَعِينَ ۝ اَمَّا بَعْدُ فَيَا عِبَادَ اللّٰهِ! اِتَّقُوا اللّٰهَ وَاَطِيعُوهُ ۝ اِنَّ اللّٰهَ مَعَ الَّذِينَ اتَّقَوْا وَالَّذِينَ هُمْ مُحْسِنُونَ ۝ قَالَ اللّٰهُ تَعَالٰى فِي كِتَابِهِ الْكَرِيمِ ۝}
$$

(Verily all praise belongs to Allah, we praise Him, seek His Aid and His Forgiveness. Whomsoever Allah guides there is none to misguide and whomsoever Allah misguides there is none to guide. I testify that there is none deserving of worship except Allah alone without any partners and I testify that Muhammad, peace and blessings be upon him, is His servant and His Messenger. O Allah, bestow Your blessings upon our master Muhammad and the Family of Muhammad, and upon his Companions. O Servants of Allah, I exhort you to fear Allah and urge you to obey Him. Verily, Allah is with those who fear and those who do good. Allah, glorified and exalted be He, said in His Holy Book:

$$\text{بِسْمِ اللهِ الرَّحْمٰنِ الرَّحِيمِ (...)}$$

$$\text{وَقَالَ النَّبِيُّ صَلَّى اللهُ عَلَيْهِ وَسَلَّمَ (...)}$$

(In the Name of Allah, the All-Merciful, the All-Compassionate, ... )

(Our noble Prophet, peace and blessings be upon him, says: …)

Later on, the sermon is delivered in the language of the mosque's community.

At the end of the first section of the sermon the following supplication is uttered:

$$\text{اَلَا اِنَّ اَحْسَنَ الْكَلَامِ وَاَبْلَغَ النِّظَامِ كَلَامُ اللهِ الْمَلِكِ الْعَزِيزِ الْعَلَّامِ ۞ كَمَا قَالَ اللهُ تَبَارَكَ وَتَعَالَى فِى الْكَلَامِ ۞ وَاِذَا قُرِئَ الْقُرْاٰنُ فَاسْتَمِعُوا لَهُ وَاَنْصِتُوا لَعَلَّكُمْ تُرْحَمُونَ. بِسْمِ اللهِ الرَّحْمٰنِ الرَّحِيمِ اِنَّ الدِّينَ عِنْدَ اللهِ الْاِسْلَامُ}$$

(Do pay attention to the fact that the most beautiful, systematic and encompassing word is the Word of the Almighty, The All-Glorious with irresistible might (Whom none can prevent from doing what He wills). Allah the Almighty stated in the Holy Qur'an: "And so, when the Qur'an is recited, give ear to it and listen in silence so that you may be shown mercy." (al-A'raf 7:204) In the Name of Allah, the All-Merciful, the All-Compassionate: "The (true) religion with Allah is Islam" (Al Imran 3:19)).

Or the following supplication is uttered:

$$\text{وَقَالَ عَلَيْهِ الصَّلَاةُ وَالسَّلَامُ التَّائِبُ مِنَ الذَّنْبِ كَمَنْ لَا ذَنْبَ لَهُ وَأَسْتَغْفِرُ اللهَ لِي وَلَكُمْ التَّوْفِيقَ}$$

(Our Prophet stated that a sin, which a person had repented from, will not be considered to have been committed. I ask forgiveness and victory from Allah the Almighty, for you and myself).

The following supplication is uttered in the pause between the first and second section of the sermon:

$$بَارَكَ اللهُ لَنَا وَلَكُمْ وَلِسَائِرِ الْمُؤْمِنِينَ وَالْمُؤْمِنَاتِ وَالْمُسْلِمِينَ وَالْمُسْلِمَاتِ اَلْاَحْيَاءِ مِنْهُمْ وَالْاَمْوَاتِ اِنَّهُ سَمِيعٌ قَرِيبٌ مُجِيبُ الدَّعَوَاتِ$$

(May Allah bless us, you and other Muslims, sisters and brothers in faith, and their kith and kin, both alive and dead! Surely, He is the One, who hears, accepts our supplications, and is the closest One to His servants!)

The following supplication is uttered in the second section of the sermon:

$$اَلْحَمْدُ لِلّٰهِ حَمْدَ الْكَامِلِينَ وَالصَّلَاةُ وَالسَّلَامُ عَلَى رَسُولِنَا مُحَمَّدٍ الْاَمِينِ وَعَلَى اٰلِهِ وَاَصْحَابِهِ اَجْمَعِينَ ۞ تَعْظِيمًا لِنَبِيِّهِ وَتَكْرِيمًا لِصَفِيِّهِ فَقَالَ عَزَّ وَجَلَّ مِنْ قَائِلٍ مُخْبِرًا وَاٰمِرًا ۞ اِنَّ اللهَ وَمَلٰئِكَتَهُ يُصَلُّونَ عَلَى النَّبِيِّ يَا اَيُّهَا الَّذِينَ اٰمَنُوا صَلُّوا عَلَيْهِ وَسَلِّمُوا تَسْلِيمًا$$

(Verily all praise belongs to Allah. May the peace and blessings of Allah be upon our Prophet Muhammad al-Amin and the Family of Muhammad, and upon all his Companions. To exalt His Messenger, the Almighty Allah says and commands in the Quran: "*Surely Allah and His angels bless the Prophet (He always treats him with His special mercy, with the angels praying to Him for the decisive victory of his religion, and granting him the highest station of praise). O you who believe, invoke the blessings of Allah on him, and pray to Allah to bestow His peace on him, greeting him with the best greeting. (Love and follow him with utmost sincerity and faithfulness, and give yourselves to his way with perfect submission).*" (al-Ahzab 33:56))

The following supplication is uttered in a lower voice:

$$اَللّٰهُمَّ صَلِّ عَلَى مُحَمَّدٍ وَعَلَى اٰلِ مُحَمَّدٍ كَمَا صَلَّيْتَ عَلَى اِبْرَاهِيمَ وَعَلَى اٰلِ اِبْرَاهِيمَ اِنَّكَ حَمِيدٌ مَجِيدٌ$$

(O Allah, bestow Your blessings upon our master Muhammad and the Family of Muhammad, as You bestowed Your blessings upon Abraham and the Family of Abraham. Assuredly, You are All-Praised, All-Illustrious).

اَللّٰهُمَّ بَارِكْ عَلٰى مُحَمَّدٍ وَعَلٰى اٰلِ مُحَمَّدٍ كَمَا بَارَكْتَ عَلٰى اِبْرَاهِيمَ وَعَلٰى اٰلِ اِبْرَاهِيمَ اِنَّكَ حَمِيدٌ مَجِيدٌ

(O Allah, send Your abundant gifts and favors unto our master Muhammad and the Family of Muhammad, as You sent them unto Abraham and the Family of Abraham. Assuredly, You are All-Praised, All-Illustrious).

اَللّٰهُمَّ وَارْضَ عَنِ الْاَرْبَعَةِ الْخُلَفَاءِ ۞ سَيِّدِنَا اَبِى بَكْرٍ وَعُمَرَ وَعُثْمَانَ وَعَلِيٍّ ذَوِى الصِّدْقِ وَالْوَفَاءِ وَبَقِيَّةِ الْعَشَرَةِ الْمُبَشَّرَةِ وَاٰلِ بَيْتِ الْمُصْطَفٰى وَعَنِ الْاَنْصَارِ وَالْمُهَاجِرِينَ وَالتَّابِعِينَ اِلٰى يَوْمِ الْجَزَاءِ ۞ اَللّٰهُمَّ اغْفِرْ لِلْمُؤْمِنِينَ وَالْمُؤْمِنَاتِ وَالْمُسْلِمِينَ وَالْمُسْلِمَاتِ الْاَحْيَاءِ مِنْهُمْ وَالْاَمْوَاتِ بِرَحْمَتِكَ يَا اَرْحَمَ الرَّاحِمِينَ ۞ وَسَلَامٌ عَلَى الْمُرْسَلِينَ وَالْحَمْدُ لِلّٰهِ رَبِّ الْعَالَمِينَ

(O Allah, be contented with our respected, loyal and faithful caliphs, Abu Bakr, Umar ibn al-Khattab, Uthman ibn Affan and Ali ibn Abi Talib, the other ten people, who were given glad tidings of entering the Paradise, people of the House (the household of Prophet Muhammad Mustafa, upon him be peace and blessings, including Fatimah, his daughter, and her husband, Ali, and their sons, Hasan and Husayn), migrants of Medina, their helpers and all those who obeyed them. O Allah, forgive all Muslim men and women, their alive and dead kith and kin with your mercy! O, the All-Merciful, the All-Compassionate One! Greetings be to all the Prophets! Praises belong to Allah, Lord of the Worlds!)

The following supplication is uttered aloud:

"O Allah, do help Muslims and the religion of Islam! Do protect our nation and people from different kinds of hazards and threats. Grant us favor in this world and in the Hereafter. Do forgive us, our parents and all other Muslims! Surely, You are the One, who hears and accepts our supplications!"

After this supplication and reciting *basmala* the following verse is recited:

اِنَّ اللهَ يَأْمُرُ بِالْعَدْلِ وَالْإِحْسَانِ وَاِيتَاءِ ذِى الْقُرْبَى وَيَنْهَى عَنِ الْفَحْشَاءِ وَالْمُنْكَرِ وَالْبَغْيِ يَعِظُكُمْ لَعَلَّكُمْ تَذَكَّرُونَ

Allah enjoins justice (and right judgment in all matters), and devotion to doing good, and generosity towards relatives; and He forbids you indecency, wickedness, and vile conduct (all offenses against religion, life, personal property, chastity, and health of mind and body). He exhorts you (repeatedly) so that you may reflect and be mindful! (an-Nahl 16:90)

## Sermon Supplication

اَلْحَمْدُ لِلّٰهِ رَبِّ الْعَالَمِينَ. وَالصَّلَاةُ وَالسَّلَامُ عَلَى رَسُولِنَا مُحَمَّدٍ وَعَلَى اٰلِهِ وَصَحْبِهِ أَجْمَعِينَ صَلُّوا عَلَي رَسُولِنَا مُحَمَّدٍ، صَلُّوا عَلَي طَبِيبِ قُلُوبِنَا مُحَمَّدٍ، صَلُّوا عَلَي شَفِيعِ ذُنُوبِنَا مُحَمَّدٍ ۞ رَبِّ اشْرَحْ لِى صَدْرِى وَيَسِّرْلِى أَمْرِى وَاحْلُلْ عُقْدَةً مِنْ لِسَانِى يَفْقَهُوا قَوْلِى وَأُفَوِّضُ أَمْرِى اِلَى اللهِ اِنَّ اللهَ بَصِيرٌ بِالْعِبَادِ سُبْحَانَكَ لَا عِلْمَ لَنَا اِلَّا مَا عَلَّمْتَنَا اِنَّكَ أَنْتَ السَّمِيعُ الْعَلِيمُ وَتُبْ عَلَيْنَا يَا مَوْلَانَا إِنَّكَ أَنْتَ التَّوَّابُ الرَّحِيمُ وَاهْدِنَا وَ وَفِّقْنَا اِلَي الْحَقِّ وَ اِلَي طَرِيقٍ مُسْتَقِيمٍ. بِبَرَكَةِ الْقُرْآنِ الْعَظِيمِ. وَ بِحُرْمَةِ مَنْ أَرْسَلْتَهُ رَحْمَةً لِلْعَالَمِينَ ۞ وَقَالَ اللهُ فِي كِتَابِهِ الْكَرِيمِ أَعُوذُ بِاللهِ مِنَ الشَّيْطَانِ الرَّجِيمِ. بِسْمِ اللهِ الرَّحْمٰنِ الرَّحِيمِ..... صَدَقَ

اللهُ العَظِيم ۞ وقَالَ رَسُولُ اللهِ صَلَّى اللهُ عَلَيْهِ وَ سَلَّمَ فِي حَدِيثِهِ الشَّرِيفِ... صَدَقَ رَسُولُ اللهِ فِيمَا قَالَ أَوْ كَمَا قَالَ

## Recitations after the Daily Prayers

After the congregational Prayers, a person, appointed by the muezzin, recites the Beautiful Names of Allah and sends blessings on the Prophet: a glorification is performed. First, the muezzin recites the following:

اَللّٰهُمَّ اَنْتَ السَّلاَمُ وَ مِنْكَ السَّلاَمُ تَبَارَكْتَ يَا ذَالْجَلاَلِ وَالْاِكْرَامِ عَلَى رَسُولِنَا صَلَوَاتٌ

(O Allah! You are the Source of Peace (and well-being), and from You comes peace, blessed and Exalted are You, Possessor of Majesty and Bounty! Blessings on our Messenger Muhammad).

Here, everyone should invoke peace and blessings upon our Prophet. Then, the muezzin will continue:

سُبْحَانَ اللهِ وَالْحَمْدُ لِلهِ وَلاَ اِلٰهَ اِلَّا اللهُ وَاللهُ اَكْبَرُ وَلاَ حَوْلَ وَلاَ قُوَّةَ اِلاَّ بِاللهِ الْعَلِيِّ الْعَظِيم

(Glory be to Allah. All Praise is for Allah. There is no deity but Allah, Allah is the Greatest. There is no might or power except with Allah).

Afterwards, everyone should silently recite the verse of the Divine Throne (al-Baqarah 2:255). Sometimes, such *surahs* as Al-Fatiha, Al-Ikhlas, Al-Falaq and An-Nas are recited. Later, the muezzin will say: *Subhan Allah* (All-Glorified is Allah) and everyone should recite *Subhan Allah* 33 times. Then the muezzin will say aloud: *Alhamdulillah* (All praise and gratitude is for Allah) and everyone should recite *Alhamdulillah* 33 times. And again, the muezzin will say aloud *Allahu Akbar* (Allah is the All-Great); here also everyone should recite *Allahu Akbar* 33 times.

Then muezzin will recite the following:

$$\text{لَا اِلٰهَ اِلَّا اللّٰهُ وَحْدَهُ لَا شَرِيكَ لَهُ لَهُ الْمُلْكُ وَلَهُ الْحَمْدُ وَهُوَ عَلٰى كُلِّ شَيْءٍ قَدِيرٌ سُبْحَانَ رَبِّيَ الْعَلِيِّ الْأَعْلَى الْوَهَّاب}$$

(There exists no deity but Allah; Allah is One, Allah has no partners; Allah has the absolute ownership and dominion; and Allah is the All-Powerful. I glorify my Lord, the All-Exalted and the All-Munificent).

Afterwards, the muezzin will open his hands and supplicate together with the community. Later, either something else will be recited or the chapter of Al-Fatiha only. However, in some places, besides this short glorification, invocations of peace and blessings upon our Prophet, and recitations of the All-Beautiful Names of Allah that are based on the *Sunnah* are recited.

## Supplication of *Adhan*

$$\text{اَللّٰهُمَّ رَبَّ هٰذِهِ الدَّعْوَةِ التَّامَّةِ وَالصَّلَاةِ الْقَائِمَةِ اٰتِ سَيِّدَنَا مُحَمَّدًا الْوَسِيلَةَ وَالْفَضِيلَةَ وَالدَّرَجَةَ الرَّفِيعَةَ وَابْعَثْهُ مَقَامًا مَحْمُودًا الَّذِي وَعَدْتَهُ إِنَّكَ لَا تُخْلِفُ الْمِيعَادَ}$$

(O Allah, Lord of this perfect call (to Prayer) and the Prayer that is about to be performed. Bestow upon our master Muhammad the right of intercession and the rank above the rest of creation, and raise him to the honored station You have promised him. Verily, You never fail in Your promise).

## Salawat Munjiyah

$$\text{اَللّٰهُمَّ صَلِّ عَلٰى سَيِّدِنَا مُحَمَّدٍ وَعَلٰى اٰلِ سَيِّدِنَا مُحَمَّدٍ صَلَاةً تُنْجِينَا بِهَا مِنْ جَمِيعِ الْأَهْوَالِ وَالْاٰفَاتِ، وَتَقْضِي لَنَا بِهَا جَمِيعَ الْحَاجَاتِ، وَتُطَهِّرُنَا بِهَا مِنْ جَمِيعِ السَّيِّئَاتِ، وَتَرْفَعُنَا بِهَا عِنْدَكَ أَعْلَى الدَّرَجَاتِ،}$$

وَتُبَلِّغُنَا بِهَا أَقْصَى الْغَايَاتِ مِنْ جَمِيعِ الْخَيْرَاتِ فِي الْحَيَاةِ وَبَعْدَ الْمَمَاتِ، اٰمِينَ يَا مُجِيبَ الدَّعَوَاتِ وَالْحَمْدُ لِلّٰهِ رَبِّ الْعَالَمِينَ

(O Allah! Bestow blessings and peace upon our master Muhammad and his Family. For the sake of that blessing and peace save us from all misfortunes and disasters, meet all of our needs, and purify us from all vices, elevate us to highest ranks in Your Sight, enable us to attain the highest of goals of all kinds of goodness in this life and the next. Amin, O Who answers all Prayers. All praise is due to Allah—Lord of the worlds).

## Salawat Tafrijiyah

اَللّٰهُمَّ صَلِّ صَلَاةً كَامِلَةً وَسَلِّمْ سَلَامًا تَامًّا عَلٰى سَيِّدِنَا مُحَمَّدٍ الَّذِي تَنْحَلُّ بِهِ الْعُقَدُ، وَتَنْفَرِجُ بِهِ الْكُرَبُ، وَتُقْضَى بِهِ الْحَوَائِجُ، وَتُنَالُ بِهِ الرَّغَائِبُ وَحُسْنُ الْخَوَاتِمِ، وَيُسْتَسْقَى الْغَمَامُ بِوَجْهِهِ الْكَرِيمِ، وَعَلٰى اٰلِهِ وَصَحْبِهِ فِي كُلِّ لَمْحَةٍ وَنَفَسٍ بِعَدَدِ كُلِّ مَعْلُومٍ لَكَ

(O Allah! Bestow complete blessings and perfect peace on our master Muhammad, and for his sake may all knots be untied (i.e., all our difficulties be removed), all calamities and agonies prevented, all needs fulfilled, all our cherished aspirations obtained, and a felicitous end to earthly life attained (with faith); and (give us) rain-showering clouds for the sake of the munificent countenance of the Prophet; and (bestow blessings as well) on his Family and Companions in every moment and every breath, as many times as is in Your Knowledge).

## Sayyidu'l-Istighfar

اَللّٰهُمَّ أَنْتَ رَبِّي لَا اِلٰهَ إِلَّا أَنْتَ خَلَقْتَنِي وَأَنَا عَبْدُكَ وَأَنَا عَلٰى عَهْدِكَ وَوَعْدِكَ مَا اسْتَطَعْتُ أَعُوذُ بِكَ مِنْ شَرِّ مَا صَنَعْتُ أَبُوءُ لَكَ بِنِعْمَتِكَ عَلَيَّ وَأَبُوءُ لَكَ بِذَنْبِي فَاغْفِرْ لِي فَإِنَّهُ لَا يَغْفِرُ الذُّنُوبَ إِلَّا أَنْتَ

(O Allah, You are my Lord, none has the right to be worshiped except You, You created me and I am Your servant and I abide by Your covenant and promise [to honor it] as best I can, I take refuge in You from the evil of which I committed, I acknowledge Your favor upon me and I acknowledge my sin, so forgive me, for verily none can forgive sins except You).

## The All-Beautiful Names of Allah

اَلْأَسْمَاءُ الْحُسْنَى

هُوَ اللهُ الَّذِي لَا إِلٰهَ إِلَّا هُوَ الرَّحْمٰنُ الرَّحِيمُ الْمَلِكُ الْقُدُّوسُ السَّلَامُ الْمُؤْمِنُ الْمُهَيْمِنُ الْعَزِيزُ الْجَبَّارُ الْمُتَكَبِّرُ الْخَالِقُ الْبَارِئُ الْمُصَوِّرُ الْغَفَّارُ الْقَهَّارُ الْوَهَّابُ الرَّزَّاقُ الْفَتَّاحُ الْعَلِيمُ الْقَابِضُ الْبَاسِطُ الْخَافِضُ الرَّافِعُ الْمُعِزُّ الْمُذِلُّ السَّمِيعُ الْبَصِيرُ الْحَكَمُ الْعَدْلُ اللَّطِيفُ الْخَبِيرُ الْحَلِيمُ الْعَظِيمُ الْغَفُورُ الشَّكُورُ الْعَلِيُّ الْكَبِيرُ الْحَفِيظُ الْمُقِيتُ الْحَسِيبُ الْجَلِيلُ الْكَرِيمُ الرَّقِيبُ الْمُجِيبُ الْوَاسِعُ الْحَكِيمُ الْوَدُودُ الْمَجِيدُ الْبَاعِثُ الشَّهِيدُ الْحَقُّ الْوَكِيلُ الْقَوِيُّ الْمَتِينُ الْوَلِيُّ الْحَمِيدُ الْمُحْصِي الْمُبْدِئُ الْمُعِيدُ الْمُحْيِي الْمُمِيتُ الْحَيُّ الْقَيُّومُ اَلْوَاجِدُ الْمَاجِدُ الْوَاحِدُ الصَّمَدُ الْقَادِرُ الْمُقْتَدِرُ الْمُقَدِّمُ الْمُؤَخِّرُ الْأَوَّلُ الْاٰخِرُ الظَّاهِرُ الْبَاطِنُ الْوَالِي الْمُتَعَالِي الْبَرُّ التَّوَّابُ اَلْمُنْتَقِمُ اَلْعَفُوُّ الرَّؤُوفُ مَالِكُ الْمُلْكِ ذُو الْجَلَالِ وَالْإِكْرَامِ الْمُقْسِطُ الْجَامِعُ الْغَنِيُّ الْمُغْنِي الْمَانِعُ الضَّارُّ النَّافِعُ النُّورُ الْهَادِي الْبَدِيعُ الْبَاقِي الْوَارِثُ الرَّشِيدُ الصَّبُورُ.

## Supplication of Food and *Iftar* (Fast-breaking Dinner)

بِسْمِ اللهِ الرَّحْمٰنِ الرَّحِيمِ كُلُوا وَشْرَبُوا وَلَا تُسْرِفُوا إِنَّهُ لَا يُحِبُّ الْمُسْرِفِينَ. اَلْحَمْدُ لِلّٰهِ الَّذِي أَطْعَمَنَا وَسَقَانَا وَجَعَلَنَا مُسْلِمِينَ. وَرَحْمَةُ اللهِ وَبَرَكَاتُهُ عَلَى صَاحِبِ الطَّعَامِ وَالْاٰكِلِينَ. اَللّٰهُمَّ زِدْ وَلَا تَنْقُصْ بِحُرْمَةِ الْفَاتِحَةِ

(In the Name of Allah, the All-Merciful, the All-Compassionate. *"Eat and drink, but do not be wasteful; indeed, He does not love the wasteful."* All praise is due to Allah Who has blessed us with food and drink and made us Muslim. May Allah's mercy and blessings be upon the host and the quests. O Allah, please increase (the blessings), and do not decrease. In honor of the secret of Surah al-Fatiha).

$$\text{بِسْمِ اللهِ الرَّحْمٰنِ الرَّحِيمِ}$$
$$\text{اَللّٰهُمَّ لَكَ صُمْتُ وَبِكَ اٰمَنْتُ وَعَلَيْكَ تَوَكَّلْتُ وَعَلَىٰ رِزْقِكَ اَفْطَرْتُ}$$

(In the Name of Allah, the All-Merciful, the All-Compassionate. O Allah, I fasted for You, believed in You, trusted You and broke my fast my Your provision!)

## Supplication of the Sacrifice

One must sacrifice an animal according to its tenet. The animal must be brought to the place of sacrifice without being dragged or troubled. It is laid down on its left side, towards the *qiblah*. Before sacrificing a sacrificial animal, the slaughterer must utter the following supplication:

$$\text{إِنِّي وَجَّهْتُ وَجْهِيَ لِلَّذِي فَطَرَ السَّمَاوَاتِ وَالْأَرْضَ}$$
$$\text{حَنِيفًا وَمَا أَنَا مِنَ الْمُشْرِكِينَ}$$

I have turned my face (my whole being) with pure faith and submission to the One Who has created the heavens and the earth, each with particular features, and I am not one of those associating partners with Allah. (al-Anam 6:79)

While slaughtering, he, along with others around, must say the *takbir* as follows:

$$\text{اَللهُ أَكْبَرُ اللهُ أَكْبَرُ لَا إِلٰهَ إِلَّا اللهُ وَاللهُ أَكْبَرُ اللهُ أَكْبَرُ وَلِلّٰهِ الْحَمْدُ}$$

After the slaughtering two units of *Shukr* (Thankfulness) Prayer are performed, where Allah the Almighty is praised and thanked. Our Prophet stated that after slaughtering the sacrificial animal, and saying two units *of Shukr*, the slaughterer must supplicate before Allah. Therefore, after completing the Prayer, the following supplication is uttered:

قُلْ إِنَّ صَلَاتِي وَنُسُكِي وَمَحْيَايَ وَمَمَاتِي لِلَّهِ رَبِّ الْعَالَمِينَ

My Prayer, and all my (other) acts and forms of devotion and worship, and my living and my dying are for Allah alone, the Lord of the worlds. (al-Anam 6:162)

# Funeral Supplications

## Supplications Made for a Dead Man

اَللَّهُمَّ اغْفِرْ لِحَيِّنَا وَمَيِّتِنَا وَذَكَرِنَا وَأُنْثَيْنَا وَصَغِيرِنَا وَكَبِيرِنَا وَشَاهِدِنَا وَغَائِبِنَا * اَللَّهُمَّ مَنْ أَحْيَيْتَهُ مِنَّا فَأَحْيِهِ عَلَى الْإِسْلَامِ وَمَنْ تَوَفَّيْتَهُ مِنَّا فَتَوَفَّهُ عَلَى الْإِيمَانِ وَخُصَّ هَذَا الْمَيِّتَ بِالرَّوْحِ وَالرَّاحَةِ وَالْمَغْفِرَةِ وَالرِّضْوَانِ * اَللَّهُمَّ إِنْ كَانَ مُحْسِنًا فَزِدْ فِي إِحْسَانِهِ وَإِنْ كَانَ مُسِيئًا فَتَجَاوَزْ عَنْهُ وَلَقِّهِ الْأَمْنَ وَالْبُشْرَى وَالْكَرَامَةَ وَالزُّلْفَى بِرَحْمَتِكَ يَا أَرْحَمَ الرَّاحِمِينَ

"O Allah! Forgive those of us that are alive and those of us that are dead; those of us that are present and those of us who are absent; those of us who are young and those of us who are adults; our males and our females. O Allah! Whomsoever You keep alive, let him live as a follower of Islam and whomsoever You cause to die, let him die a Believer. O Allah! Grant him protection, and have mercy on him, and keep him in good condition, pardon him, and be pleased with him. O Allah, if this person is a possessor of virtue, then increase his bounties. O the All-Compassionate and All-Merciful, if this person is a sinner, then forgive his sins; give him trust, joy and goodness!"

## Supplications Made for a Dead Woman

The pronouns are simply changed:

اَللّٰهُمَّ اغْفِرْ لِحَيِّنَا وَمَيِّتِنَا وَذَكَرِنَا وَأُنْثِيَانَا وَصَغِيرِنَا وَكَبِيرِنَا وَشَاهِدِنَا وَغَائِبِنَا ۞ اَللّٰهُمَّ مَنْ أَحْيَيْتَهُ مِنَّا فَأَحْيِهِ عَلَى الْإِسْلَامِ وَمَنْ تَوَفَّيْتَهُ مِنَّا فَتَوَفَّهُ عَلَى الْإِيمَانِ وَخُصَّ هٰذِهِ الْمَيِّتَةَ بِالرَّوْحِ وَالرَّاحَةِ وَالْمَغْفِرَةِ وَالرِّضْوَانِ ۞ اَللّٰهُمَّ إِنْ كَانَتْ مُحْسِنَةً فَزِدْ فِي إِحْسَانِهَا وَإِنْ كَانَتْ مُسِيئَةً فَتَجَاوَزْ عَنْهَا وَلَقِّهَا الْأَمْنَ وَالْبُشْرَى وَالْكَرَامَةَ وَالزُّلْفَى بِرَحْمَتِكَ يَا أَرْحَمَ الرَّاحِمِينَ

## Supplications Made for a Dead Boy

اَللّٰهُمَّ اغْفِرْ لِحَيِّنَا وَمَيِّتِنَا وَذَكَرِنَا وَأُنْثِيَانَا وَصَغِيرِنَا وَكَبِيرِنَا وَشَاهِدِنَا وَغَائِبِنَا ۞ اَللّٰهُمَّ مَنْ أَحْيَيْتَهُ مِنَّا فَأَحْيِهِ عَلَى الْإِسْلَامِ وَمَنْ تَوَفَّيْتَهُ مِنَّا فَتَوَفَّهُ عَلَى الْإِيمَانِ ۞ اَللّٰهُمَّ اجْعَلْهُ لَنَا فَرَطًا ، وَاجْعَلْهُ لَنَا أَجْرًا وَذُخْرًا ، وَاجْعَلْهُ لَنَا شَافِعًا مُشَفَّعًا

"O Allah! Forgive those of us that are alive and those of us that are dead; those of us that are present and those of us who are absent; those of us who are young and those of us who are adults; our males and our females. O Allah! Whomsoever You keep alive, let him live as a follower of Islam and whomsoever You cause to die, let him die a Believer. O Allah, make this as a means of Your reward (sent from the very beginning), make him as a provision of ours, let him be an intercessor of ours and accept his intercession!"

## Supplications Made for a Dead Girl

The pronouns are simply changed:

اَللّٰهُمَّ اغْفِرْ لِحَيِّنَا وَمَيِّتِنَا وَذَكَرِنَا وَأُنْثِيَانَا وَصَغِيرِنَا وَكَبِيرِنَا وَشَاهِدِنَا وَغَائِبِنَا ۞ اَللّٰهُمَّ مَنْ أَحْيَيْتَهُ مِنَّا فَأَحْيِهِ عَلَى الْإِسْلَامِ وَمَنْ تَوَفَّيْتَهُ مِنَّا

فَتَوَفَّهُ عَلَى الْإِيْمَانِ ۞ اَللَّهُمَّ اجْعَلْهَا لَنَا فَرَطًا وَاجْعَلْهَا لَنَا أَجْرًا وَذُخْرًا وَاجْعَلْهَا لَنَا شَافِعًا مُشَفَّعًا

## Supplication of a Graveyard Visit

اَلسَّلَامُ عَلَيْكُمْ أَهْلَ الدِّيَارِ مِنَ الْمُؤْمِنِينَ وَالْمُسْلِمِينَ، وَإِنَّا إِنْ شَآءَ اللهُ بِكُمْ لَلاحِقُونَ، نَسْأَلُ اللهَ لَنَا وَلَكُمُ الْعَافِيَةَ، أَنْتُمْ لَنَا فَرَطٌ وَنَحْنُ لَكُمْ تَبَعٌ وَيَرْحَمُ اللهُ الْمُسْتَقْدِمِينَ وَالْمُسْتَأْخِرِينَ

"Greetings to you o believers and those who were buried in lands of Muslims! Soon, by Allah's will, we, too, will join you. May Allah bestow deliverance to you and to us! You all passed over before us. We are those who will come after you. May Allah forgive those who went before and who will come after!"

## Supplication of Recitation of the Whole Qur'an (Khatm al-Qur'an)

بِسْمِ اللهِ الرَّحْمٰنِ الرَّحِيمِ

اَلْحَمْدُ لِلّٰهِ رَبِّ الْعَالَمِينَ. الرَّحْمٰنِ الرَّحِيمِ. مَالِكِ يَوْمِ الدِّينِ. إِيَّاكَ نَعْبُدُ وَإِيَّاكَ نَسْتَعِينُ. اهْدِنَا الصِّرَاطَ الْمُسْتَقِيمَ. صِرَاطَ الَّذِينَ أَنْعَمْتَ عَلَيْهِمْ، غَيْرِ الْمَغْضُوبِ عَلَيْهِمْ وَلَا الضَّآلِّينَ ۞ الٓمٓ. ذٰلِكَ الْكِتَابُ لَا رَيْبَ فِيهِ، هُدًى لِلْمُتَّقِينَ. الَّذِينَ يُؤْمِنُونَ بِالْغَيْبِ وَيُقِيمُونَ الصَّلٰوةَ وَمِمَّا رَزَقْنَاهُمْ يُنْفِقُونَ. وَالَّذِينَ يُؤْمِنُونَ بِمَآ أُنْزِلَ إِلَيْكَ وَمَآ أُنْزِلَ مِنْ قَبْلِكَ، وَبِالْآخِرَةِ هُمْ يُوقِنُونَ. أُولٰئِكَ عَلٰى هُدًى مِنْ رَبِّهِمْ وَأُولٰئِكَ هُمُ الْمُفْلِحُونَ ۞ اٰمَنَ الرَّسُولُ بِمَآ أُنْزِلَ إِلَيْهِ مِنْ رَبِّهِ وَالْمُؤْمِنُونَ، كُلٌّ اٰمَنَ بِاللهِ وَمَلٰئِكَتِهِ وَكُتُبِهِ وَرُسُلِهِ، لَا نُفَرِّقُ

بَيْنَ أَحَدٍ مِنْ رُسُلِهِ، وَقَالُوا سَمِعْنَا وَأَطَعْنَا غُفْرَانَكَ رَبَّنَا وَإِلَيْكَ الْمَصِيرُ. لاَ يُكَلِّفُ اللهُ نَفْسًا إِلاَّ وُسْعَهَا، لَهَا مَا كَسَبَتْ وَعَلَيْهَا مَا اكْتَسَبَتْ. رَبَّنَا لاَ تُؤَاخِذْنَا إِنْ نَسِينَا أَوْ أَخْطَأْنَا، رَبَّنَا وَلاَ تَحْمِلْ عَلَيْنَا إِصْرًا كَمَا حَمَلْتَهُ عَلَى الَّذِينَ مِنْ قَبْلِنَا، رَبَّنَا وَلاَ تُحَمِّلْنَا مَا لاَ طَاقَةَ لَنَا بِهِ، وَاعْفُ عَنَّا، وَاغْفِرْ لَنَا، وَارْحَمْنَا، أَنْتَ مَوْلاَنَا فَانْصُرْنَا عَلَى الْقَوْمِ الْكَافِرِينَ ۞ رَبَّنَا تَقَبَّلْ مِنَّا إِنَّكَ أَنْتَ السَّمِيعُ الْعَلِيمُ. رَبَّنَا وَاجْعَلْنَا مُسْلِمَيْنِ لَكَ وَمِنْ ذُرِّيَّتِنَا أُمَّةً مُسْلِمَةً لَكَ. وَأَرِنَا مَنَاسِكَنَا وَتُبْ عَلَيْنَا إِنَّكَ أَنْتَ التَّوَّابُ الرَّحِيمُ. رَبَّنَا وَابْعَثْ فِيهِمْ رَسُولاً مِنْهُمْ يَتْلُوا عَلَيْهِمْ آيَاتِكَ وَيُعَلِّمُهُمُ الْكِتَابَ وَالْحِكْمَةَ وَيُزَكِّيهِمْ، إِنَّكَ أَنْتَ الْعَزِيزُ الْحَكِيمُ. رَبَّنَا آتِنَا فِي الدُّنْيَا حَسَنَةً وَفِي الْآخِرَةِ حَسَنَةً وَقِنَا عَذَابَ النَّارِ. رَبَّنَا أَفْرِغْ عَلَيْنَا صَبْرًا وَثَبِّتْ أَقْدَامَنَا وَانْصُرْنَا عَلَى الْقَوْمِ الْكَافِرِينَ. رَبَّنَا لاَ تُزِغْ قُلُوبَنَا بَعْدَ إِذْ هَدَيْتَنَا وَهَبْ لَنَا مِنْ لَدُنْكَ رَحْمَةً، إِنَّكَ أَنْتَ الْوَهَّابُ. رَبَّنَا إِنَّكَ جَامِعُ النَّاسِ لِيَوْمٍ لاَ رَيْبَ فِيهِ، إِنَّ اللهَ لاَ يُخْلِفُ الْمِيعَادَ. رَبَّنَا إِنَّنَا آمَنَّا فَاغْفِرْ لَنَا ذُنُوبَنَا وَقِنَا عَذَابَ النَّارِ. رَبَّنَا آمَنَّا بِمَا أَنْزَلْتَ وَاتَّبَعْنَا الرَّسُولَ فَاكْتُبْنَا مَعَ الشَّاهِدِينَ. رَبَّنَا اغْفِرْ لَنَا ذُنُوبَنَا وَإِسْرَافَنَا فِي أَمْرِنَا وَثَبِّتْ أَقْدَامَنَا وَانْصُرْنَا عَلَى الْقَوْمِ الْكَافِرِينَ. رَبَّنَا إِنَّنَا سَمِعْنَا مُنَادِيًا يُنَادِي لِلْإِيمَانِ أَنْ آمِنُوا بِرَبِّكُمْ فَآمَنَّا. رَبَّنَا فَاغْفِرْ لَنَا ذُنُوبَنَا وَكَفِّرْ عَنَّا سَيِّئَاتِنَا وَتَوَفَّنَا مَعَ الْأَبْرَارِ. رَبَّنَا وَآتِنَا مَا وَعَدْتَنَا عَلَى رُسُلِكَ وَلاَ تُخْزِنَا يَوْمَ الْقِيَامَةِ، إِنَّكَ لاَ تُخْلِفُ الْمِيعَادَ. رَبَّنَا آمَنَّا فَاكْتُبْنَا مَعَ الشَّاهِدِينَ. رَبَّنَا ظَلَمْنَا أَنْفُسَنَا وَإِنْ لَمْ تَغْفِرْ لَنَا وَتَرْحَمْنَا لَنَكُونَنَّ مِنَ الْخَاسِرِينَ. رَبَّنَا لاَ تَجْعَلْنَا مَعَ الْقَوْمِ الظَّالِمِينَ.

رَبَّنَا افْتَحْ بَيْنَنَا وَبَيْنَ قَوْمِنَا بِالْحَقِّ وَأَنْتَ خَيْرُ الْفَاتِحِينَ. رَبَّنَا أَفْرِغْ عَلَيْنَا صَبْرًا وَتَوَفَّنَا مُسْلِمِينَ. رَبَّنَا لَا تَجْعَلْنَا فِتْنَةً لِلْقَوْمِ الظَّالِمِينَ. وَنَجِّنَا بِرَحْمَتِكَ مِنَ الْقَوْمِ الْكَافِرِينَ. رَبِّ اجْعَلْنِي مُقِيمَ الصَّلَاةِ وَمِنْ ذُرِّيَّتِي، رَبَّنَا وَتَقَبَّلْ دُعَاءِ. رَبَّنَا اغْفِرْ لِي وَلِوَالِدَيَّ وَلِلْمُؤْمِنِينَ يَوْمَ يَقُومُ الْحِسَابُ. رَبِّ أَدْخِلْنِي مُدْخَلَ صِدْقٍ وَأَخْرِجْنِي مُخْرَجَ صِدْقٍ وَاجْعَلْ لِي مِنْ لَدُنْكَ سُلْطَانًا نَصِيرًا. رَبَّنَا آتِنَا مِنْ لَدُنْكَ رَحْمَةً وَهَيِّئْ لَنَا مِنْ أَمْرِنَا رَشَدًا. رَبِّ اشْرَحْ لِي صَدْرِي، وَيَسِّرْ لِي أَمْرِي، وَاحْلُلْ عُقْدَةً مِنْ لِسَانِي يَفْقَهُوا قَوْلِي. رَبِّ زِدْنِي عِلْمًا. رَبِّ لَا تَذَرْنِي فَرْدًا وَأَنْتَ خَيْرُ الْوَارِثِينَ. رَبِّ أَنْزِلْنِي مُنْزَلًا مُبَارَكًا وَأَنْتَ خَيْرُ الْمُنْزِلِينَ. رَبِّ انْصُرْنِي بِمَا كَذَّبُونِ. رَبِّ فَلَا تَجْعَلْنِي فِي الْقَوْمِ الظَّالِمِينَ. رَبِّ أَعُوذُ بِكَ مِنْ هَمَزَاتِ الشَّيَاطِينِ. وَأَعُوذُ بِكَ رَبِّ أَنْ يَحْضُرُونِ. رَبَّنَا آمَنَّا فَاغْفِرْ لَنَا وَارْحَمْنَا وَأَنْتَ خَيْرُ الرَّاحِمِينَ. رَبِّ اغْفِرْ وَارْحَمْ وَأَنْتَ خَيْرُ الرَّاحِمِينَ. رَبَّنَا اصْرِفْ عَنَّا عَذَابَ جَهَنَّمَ، إِنَّ عَذَابَهَا كَانَ غَرَامًا. إِنَّهَا سَاءَتْ مُسْتَقَرًّا وَمُقَامًا. رَبَّنَا هَبْ لَنَا مِنْ أَزْوَاجِنَا وَذُرِّيَّاتِنَا قُرَّةَ أَعْيُنٍ، وَاجْعَلْنَا لِلْمُتَّقِينَ إِمَامًا. رَبِّ هَبْ لِي حُكْمًا وَأَلْحِقْنِي بِالصَّالِحِينَ. رَبِّ أَوْزِعْنِي أَنْ أَشْكُرَ نِعْمَتَكَ الَّتِي أَنْعَمْتَ عَلَيَّ وَعَلَى وَالِدَيَّ وَأَنْ أَعْمَلَ صَالِحًا تَرْضَاهُ وَأَدْخِلْنِي بِرَحْمَتِكَ فِي عِبَادِكَ الصَّالِحِينَ. رَبِّ إِنِّي ظَلَمْتُ نَفْسِي فَاغْفِرْ لِي. رَبِّ بِمَا أَنْعَمْتَ عَلَيَّ فَلَنْ أَكُونَ ظَهِيرًا لِلْمُجْرِمِينَ. رَبِّ نَجِّنِي مِنَ الْقَوْمِ الظَّالِمِينَ. رَبِّ إِنِّي لِمَا أَنْزَلْتَ إِلَيَّ مِنْ خَيْرٍ فَقِيرٌ. رَبِّ انْصُرْنِي عَلَى الْقَوْمِ الْمُفْسِدِينَ. رَبِّ هَبْ لِي مِنَ الصَّالِحِينَ. رَبَّنَا وَسِعْتَ

كُلَّ شَيْءٍ رَحْمَةً وَعِلْمًا، فَاغْفِرْ لِلَّذِينَ تَابُوا وَاتَّبَعُوا سَبِيلَكَ وَقِهِمْ عَذَابَ الْجَحِيمِ. رَبَّنَا وَأَدْخِلْهُمْ جَنَّاتِ عَدْنٍ الَّتِي وَعَدْتَهُمْ وَمَنْ صَلَحَ مِنْ آبَائِهِمْ وَأَزْوَاجِهِمْ وَذُرِّيَّاتِهِمْ، إِنَّكَ أَنْتَ الْعَزِيزُ الْحَكِيمُ. رَبَّنَا اكْشِفْ عَنَّا الْعَذَابَ إِنَّا مُؤْمِنُونَ. رَبِّ أَوْزِعْنِي أَنْ أَشْكُرَ نِعْمَتَكَ الَّتِي أَنْعَمْتَ عَلَيَّ وَعَلَى وَالِدَيَّ وَأَنْ أَعْمَلَ صَالِحًا تَرْضَاهُ وَأَصْلِحْ لِي فِي ذُرِّيَّتِي، إِنِّي تُبْتُ إِلَيْكَ وَإِنِّي مِنَ الْمُسْلِمِينَ. رَبَّنَا اغْفِرْ لَنَا وَلِإِخْوَانِنَا الَّذِينَ سَبَقُونَا بِالْإِيمَانِ، وَلَا تَجْعَلْ فِي قُلُوبِنَا غِلًّا لِلَّذِينَ آمَنُوا، رَبَّنَا إِنَّكَ رَؤُوفٌ رَحِيمٌ. رَبَّنَا عَلَيْكَ تَوَكَّلْنَا وَإِلَيْكَ أَنَبْنَا وَإِلَيْكَ الْمَصِيرُ. رَبَّنَا لَا تَجْعَلْنَا فِتْنَةً لِلَّذِينَ كَفَرُوا، وَاغْفِرْ لَنَا رَبَّنَا إِنَّكَ أَنْتَ الْعَزِيزُ الْحَكِيمُ. رَبَّنَا أَتْمِمْ لَنَا نُورَنَا وَاغْفِرْ لَنَا إِنَّكَ عَلَى كُلِّ شَيْءٍ قَدِيرٌ. رَبِّ اغْفِرْ لِي وَلِوَالِدَيَّ وَلِمَنْ دَخَلَ بَيْتِيَ مُؤْمِنًا وَلِلْمُؤْمِنِينَ وَالْمُؤْمِنَاتِ وَلَا تَزِدِ الظَّالِمِينَ إِلَّا تَبَارًا ۞ اَلْحَمْدُ للهِ حَمْدًا يُوَافِي نِعَمَهُ وَيُكَافِئُ مَزِيدَهُ وَيَدْفَعُ عَنَّا بَلَاءَهُ وَنِقَمَهُ. يَا رَبَّنَا لَكَ الْحَمْدُ كَمَا يَنْبَغِي لِجَلَالِ وَجْهِكَ وَعَظِيمِ سُلْطَانِكَ وَمَجْدِكَ. اللَّهُمَّ أَصْلِحْ قُلُوبَنَا، وَأَزِلْ عُيُوبَنَا، وَتَوَلَّنَا بِالْحُسْنَى، وَزَيِّنَّا بِالتَّقْوَى، وَاجْمَعْ لَنَا خَيْرَ الْآخِرَةِ وَالْأُولَى. اللَّهُمَّ يَا بَاسِطَ الْيَدَيْنِ بِالْعَطِيَّةِ وَالْإِجَابَةِ لِعِبَادِهِ، وَيَا صَاحِبَ الْمَوَاهِبِ وَالْعَطْفِ وَالرَّأْفَةِ عَلَى خَلْقِهِ، نَسْأَلُكَ اللَّهُمَّ أَنْ تُصَلِّيَ وَتُسَلِّمَ عَلَى عَبْدِكَ وَرَسُولِكَ سَيِّدِنَا مُحَمَّدٍ كَمَا صَلَّيْتَ عَلَى إِبْرَاهِيمَ وَعَلَى آلِ إِبْرَاهِيمَ إِنَّكَ حَمِيدٌ مَجِيدٌ. اللَّهُمَّ إِنَّا عَبِيدُكَ بَنُو عَبِيدِكَ بَنُو إِمَائِكَ، نَوَاصِينَا بِيَدِكَ، مَاضٍ فِينَا حُكْمُكَ، عَدْلٌ فِينَا قَضَاؤُكَ، نَسْأَلُكَ بِكُلِّ اسْمٍ هُوَ لَكَ سَمَّيْتَ بِهِ نَفْسَكَ أَوْ أَنْزَلْتَهُ فِي كِتَابِكَ

Religious Oratory and Supplication 79

أَوْ عَلَّمْتَهُ أَحَدًا مِنْ خَلْقِكَ أَوِ اسْتَأْثَرْتَ بِهِ فِي عِلْمِ الْغَيْبِ عِنْدَكَ، أَنْ تَجْعَلَ الْقُرْآنَ الْعَظِيمَ رَبِيعَ قُلُوبِنَا وَنُورَ أَبْصَارِنَا وَجِلَاءَ حُزْنِنَا وَذَهَابَ هَمِّنَا وَغَمِّنَا يَا أَرْحَمَ الرَّاحِمِينَ. اللَّهُمَّ اجْعَلِ الْقُرْآنَ الْكَرِيمَ لَنَا إِمَامًا وَنُورًا وَهُدًى وَرَحْمَةً، وَلَا تَجْعَلْهُ عَلَيْنَا وَبَالًا وَغَضَبًا وَنِقْمَةً. اللَّهُمَّ ذَكِّرْنَا مِنْهُ مَا نَسِينَاهُ، وَعَلِّمْنَا مِنْهُ مَا جَهِلْنَاهُ، وَارْزُقْنَا تِلَاوَتَهُ وَفَهْمَ مَعْنَاهُ مَعَ الْعَمَلِ بِهِ آنَاءَ اللَّيْلِ وَأَطْرَافَ النَّهَارِ لَعَلَّكَ تَرْضَى، وَاجْعَلْهُ حُجَّةً لَنَا وَلَا تَجْعَلْهُ حُجَّةً عَلَيْنَا، وَاجْعَلْنَا مِمَّنْ يَقْرَؤُهُ فَيَرْقَى، وَلَا تَجْعَلْنَا مِمَّنْ يَقْرَؤُهُ فَيَذِلَّ وَيَشْقَى. اللَّهُمَّ إِنَّا نَسْتَوْدِعُكَ دِينَنَا وَأَنْفُسَنَا وَأَهْلِينَا وَخَوَاتِيمَ أَعْمَالِنَا. اللَّهُمَّ إِنَّا نَسْأَلُكَ إِيمَانًا لَا يَرْتَدُّ، وَنَعِيمًا لَا يَنْفَدُ، وَقُرَّةَ عَيْنٍ لَا تَنْقَطِعُ، وَلَذَّةَ النَّظَرِ إِلَى وَجْهِكَ الْكَرِيمِ وَمُرَافَقَةَ نَبِيِّنَا مُحَمَّدٍ صَلَّى اللهُ عَلَيْهِ وَسَلَّمَ فِي جَنَّاتِ النَّعِيمِ. اللَّهُمَّ ارْحَمْنَا بِتَرْكِ الْمَعَاصِي أَبَدًا مَا أَبْقَيْتَنَا، وَارْحَمْنَا أَنْ نَتَكَلَّفَ مَا لَا يَعْنِينَا، وَارْزُقْنَا حُسْنَ النَّظَرِ فِيمَا يُرْضِيكَ عَنَّا. اللَّهُمَّ بَدِيعَ السَّمَوَاتِ وَالْأَرْضِ ذَا الْجَلَالِ وَالْإِكْرَامِ، وَالْعِزَّةِ الَّتِي لَا تُرَامُ، نَسْأَلُكَ يَا اللهُ يَا رَحْمَنُ يَا رَحِيمُ بِجَلَالِكَ وَنُورِ وَجْهِكَ أَنْ تُلْزِمَ قُلُوبَنَا حِفْظَ كِتَابِكَ كَمَا عَلَّمْتَنَا، وَارْزُقْنَا أَنْ نَتْلُوَهُ عَلَى النَّحْوِ الَّذِي يُرْضِيكَ عَنَّا. اللَّهُمَّ بَدِيعَ السَّمَوَاتِ وَالْأَرْضِ ذَا الْجَلَالِ وَالْإِكْرَامِ وَالْعِزَّةِ الَّتِي لَا تُرَامُ، نَسْأَلُكَ يَا اللهُ يَا رَحْمَنُ بِجَلَالِكَ وَنُورِ وَجْهِكَ أَنْ تُنَوِّرَ بِكِتَابِكَ أَبْصَارَنَا، وَأَنْ تُطْلِقَ بِهِ أَلْسِنَتَنَا، وَأَنْ تُفَرِّجَ بِهِ عَنْ قُلُوبِنَا، وَأَنْ تَشْرَحَ بِهِ صُدُورَنَا، وَأَنْ تَسْتَعْمِلَ بِهِ أَبْدَانَنَا، فَإِنَّهُ لَا يُعِينُنَا عَلَى الْحَقِّ غَيْرُكَ، وَلَا يُؤْتِينَاهُ إِلَّا أَنْتَ. وَلَا حَوْلَ وَلَا قُوَّةَ إِلَّا بِاللهِ الْعَلِيِّ الْعَظِيمِ.

اَللّٰهُمَّ إِنَّا نَسْأَلُكَ رَحْمَةً مِنْ عِنْدِكَ تَهْدِي بِهَا قُلُوبَنَا، وَتَجْمَعُ بِهَا أُمُورَنَا، وَتَلُمُّ بِهَا شَعَثَنَا، وَتُصْلِحُ بِهَا شَأْنَنَا، وَتَحْفَظُ بِهَا غَائِبَنَا، وَتُزَكِّي بِهَا عَمَلَنَا، وَتُلْهِمُنَا بِهَا رُشْدَنَا، وَتَرُدُّ بِهَا أُلْفَتَنَا، وَتَعْصِمُنَا بِهَا مِنْ كُلِّ سُوءٍ. اَللّٰهُمَّ فَارِجَ الْهَمِّ، كَاشِفَ الْغَمِّ، مُجِيبَ دَعْوَةِ الْمُضْطَرِّينَ، رَحْمٰنَ الدُّنْيَا وَالْآخِرَةِ وَرَحِيمَهُمَا، ارْحَمْنَا بِرَحْمَةٍ تُغْنِينَا بِهَا عَنْ رَحْمَةِ مَنْ سِوَاكَ. اَللّٰهُمَّ أَغْنِنَا بِحَلَالِكَ عَنْ حَرَامِكَ، وَبِطَاعَتِكَ عَنْ مَعْصِيَتِكَ، وَاكْفِنَا بِفَضْلِكَ وَجُودِكَ وَكَرَمِكَ عَمَّنْ سِوَاكَ. اَللّٰهُمَّ إِنَّكَ تَعْلَمُ سِرَّنَا وَعَلَانِيَتَنَا فَاقْبَلْ مَعْذِرَتَنَا، وَتَعْلَمُ حَاجَاتِنَا فَأَعْطِنَا سُؤْلَنَا، وَتَعْلَمُ مَا فِي نُفُوسِنَا فَاغْفِرْ لَنَا ذُنُوبَنَا. اَللّٰهُمَّ إِنَّا نَسْأَلُكَ إِيمَانًا يُبَاشِرُ قُلُوبَنَا، وَيَقِينًا صَادِقًا حَتَّى نَعْلَمَ أَنَّهُ لَا يُصِيبُنَا إِلَّا مَا كَتَبْتَهُ عَلَيْنَا، وَالرِّضَا بِمَا قَسَمْتَهُ لَنَا يَا ذَا الْجَلَالِ وَالْإِكْرَامِ. اَللّٰهُمَّ إِنَّا نَسْأَلُكَ مُوجِبَاتِ رَحْمَتِكَ، وَعَزَائِمَ مَغْفِرَتِكَ، وَالسَّلَامَةَ مِنْ كُلِّ إِثْمٍ، وَالْغَنِيمَةَ مِنْ كُلِّ بِرٍّ، وَنَسْأَلُكَ الْفَوْزَ بِالْجَنَّةِ وَالنَّجَاةَ مِنَ النَّارِ. اَللّٰهُمَّ اقْسِمْ لَنَا مِنْ خَشْيَتِكَ مَا تَحُولُ بِهِ بَيْنَنَا وَبَيْنَ مَعَاصِيكَ، وَمِنْ طَاعَتِكَ مَا تُبَلِّغُنَا بِهِ جَنَّتَكَ، وَمِنَ الْيَقِينِ مَا تُهَوِّنُ بِهِ عَلَيْنَا مَصَائِبَ الدُّنْيَا، وَمَتِّعْنَا اَللّٰهُمَّ بِأَسْمَاعِنَا وَأَبْصَارِنَا وَقُوَّتِنَا مَا أَحْيَيْتَنَا، وَاجْعَلْهُ الْوَارِثَ مِنَّا، وَاجْعَلْ ثَأْرَنَا عَلَى مَنْ ظَلَمَنَا، وَانْصُرْنَا عَلَى مَنْ عَادَانَا، وَلَا تَجْعَلْ مُصِيبَتَنَا فِي دِينِنَا، وَلَا تَجْعَلِ الدُّنْيَا أَكْبَرَ هَمِّنَا، وَلَا مَبْلَغَ عِلْمِنَا، وَلَا تُسَلِّطْ عَلَيْنَا بِذُنُوبِنَا مَنْ لَا يَخَافُكَ وَلَا يَرْحَمُنَا، وَكُفَّ أَيْدِيَ الظَّالِمِينَ عَنَّا، بِرَحْمَتِكَ يَا أَرْحَمَ الرَّاحِمِينَ. اَللّٰهُمَّ اجْعَلْنَا مِمَّنْ سَبَقَتْ لَهُمْ مِنْكَ الْحُسْنَى وَزِيَادَةٌ. اَللّٰهُمَّ أَغْنِنَا بِالْعِلْمِ، وَزَيِّنَّا

بِالْحِلْمِ، وَأَكْرِمْنَا بِالتَّقْوَى، وَجَمِّلْنَا بِالْعَافِيَةِ. اَللَّهُمَّ عَلِّمْنَا مَا يَنْفَعُنَا وَانْفَعْنَا بِمَا عَلَّمْتَنَا، وَزِدْنَا عِلْمًا. اَلْحَمْدُ لِلَّهِ عَلَى كُلِّ حَالٍ، وَنَعُوذُ بِاللهِ مِنْ حَالِ أَهْلِ النَّارِ. اَللَّهُمَّ اجْعَلْ جَمْعَنَا هَذَا جَمْعًا مَرْحُومًا، وَتَفَرُّقَنَا مِنْ بَعْدِهِ تَفَرُّقًا مَعْصُومًا، وَلَا تَجْعَلْ فِينَا وَلَا مَعَنَا شَقِيًّا وَلَا مَطْرُودًا وَلَا مَحْرُومًا، بِرَحْمَتِكَ يَا أَرْحَمَ الرَّاحِمِينَ، يَا حَيُّ يَا قَيُّومُ، بِرَحْمَتِكَ نَسْتَغِيثُ، وَمِنْ عَذَابِكَ نَسْتَجِيرُ، أَصْلِحْ لَنَا شَأْنَنَا كُلَّهُ، وَلَا تَكِلْنَا إِلَى أَنْفُسِنَا طَرْفَةَ عَيْنٍ. اَللَّهُمَّ أَوْصِلْ ثَوَابَ مَا قَرَأْنَاهُ مِنَ الْقُرْآنِ الْعَظِيمِ إِلَى نَبِيِّكَ وَحَبِيبِكَ وَصَفْوَتِكَ مِنْ خَلْقِكَ سَيِّدِنَا وَمَوْلَانَا مُحَمَّدٍ وَإِلَى آلِهِ وَأَصْحَابِهِ وَأَزْوَاجِهِ وَذُرِّيَّتِهِ يَا رَبَّ الْعَالَمِينَ، وَنَسْأَلُكَ اللَّهُمَّ أَنْ تَجْعَلَ ثَوَابَ مَا قَرَأْنَاهُ مِنَ الْقُرْآنِ الْعَظِيمِ إِلَى آبَائِنَا وَأُمَّهَاتِنَا وَمَشَايِخِنَا وَأَزْوَاجِنَا وَأَوْلَادِنَا وَإِخْوَانِنَا الْمُسْلِمِينَ، الَّذِينَ سَبَقُونَا بِالْإِيمَانِ، وَضَاعِفْ رَحْمَتَكَ وَرِضْوَانَكَ عَلَيْهِمْ. اللَّهُمَّ أَحِلَّ أَرْوَاحَهُمْ فِي مَحَلِّ الْأَبْرَارِ، وَتَغَمَّدْهُمْ بِالرَّحْمَةِ آنَاءَ اللَّيْلِ وَأَطْرَافَ النَّهَارِ، بِرَحْمَتِكَ يَا أَرْحَمَ الرَّاحِمِينَ. اَللَّهُمَّ انْقُلْهُمْ مِنْ ضِيقِ اللُّحُودِ وَالْقُبُورِ إِلَى سَعَةِ الدُّورِ وَالْقُصُورِ، فِي سِدْرٍ مَخْضُودٍ، وَطَلْحٍ مَنْضُودٍ، وَظِلٍّ مَمْدُودٍ، وَمَاءٍ مَسْكُوبٍ، وَفَاكِهَةٍ كَثِيرَةٍ، لَا مَقْطُوعَةٍ وَلَا مَمْنُوعَةٍ، مَعَ الَّذِينَ أَنْعَمْتَ عَلَيْهِمْ مِنَ النَّبِيِّينَ وَالصِّدِّيقِينَ وَالشُّهَدَاءِ وَالصَّالِحِينَ، بِرَحْمَتِكَ يَا أَرْحَمَ الرَّاحِمِينَ. اَللَّهُمَّ اجْعَلْنَا وَإِيَّاهُمْ مِنْ عِبَادِكَ الَّذِينَ تُبَاهِي بِهِمْ مَلَائِكَتَكَ فِي الدُّنْيَا وَالْآخِرَةِ، وَارْزُقْنَا وَإِيَّاهُمْ حُسْنَ النَّظَرِ إِلَى وَجْهِكَ الْكَرِيمِ مَعَ الْفَائِزِينَ بِرَحْمَتِكَ وَرِضْوَانِكَ مِنْ عِبَادِكَ الَّذِينَ تَجْرِي مِنْ تَحْتِهِمُ الْأَنْهَارُ فِي جَنَّاتِ النَّعِيمِ.

دَعْوَاهُمْ فِيهَا سُبْحَانَكَ اللَّهُمَّ وَتَحِيَّتُهُمْ فِيهَا سَلَامٌ. اَللَّهُمَّ أَصْلِحْ وُلَاةَ الْمُسْلِمِينَ وَوَفِّقْهُمْ لِلْعَدْلِ فِي رَعَايَاهُمْ وَالْإِحْسَانِ إِلَيْهِمْ وَالشَّفَقَةِ عَلَيْهِمْ، وَالرِّفْقِ بِهِمْ، وَالْعِنَايَةِ بِمَصَالِحِهِمْ، وَحَبِّبْهُمْ إِلَى الرَّعِيَّةِ وَحَبِّبْ الرَّعِيَّةَ إِلَيْهِمْ، وَارْزُقْهُمْ الْبِطَانَةَ الصَّالِحَةَ الَّتِي تَهْدِيهِمْ إِلَى الْحَقِّ وَالْخَيْرِ، وَتُعِينُهُمْ عَلَيْهِ، وَوَفِّقْهُمْ إِلَى صِرَاطِكَ الْمُسْتَقِيمِ، وَإِلَى الْعَمَلِ بِأَحْكَامِ دِينِكَ الْقَوِيمِ، إِنَّكَ أَنْتَ السَّمِيعُ الْعَلِيمُ. اَللَّهُمَّ بَارِكْ وَاغْفِرْ وَارْحَمْ لِمَنْ قَامَ عَلَى خِدْمَةِ كِتَابِكَ الْعَزِيزِ، تِلَاوَةً وَإِنْفَاقًا وَطِبَاعَةً وَمُرَاجَعَةً، وَاجْعَلْهُ عَمَلًا خَالِصًا لِوَجْهِكَ الْكَرِيمِ، إِنَّكَ سَمِيعٌ مُجِيبٌ. وَآخِرُ دَعْوَانَا أَنِ الْحَمْدُ لِلَّهِ رَبِّ الْعَالَمِينَ ۞ وَصَلَّى اللهُ وَسَلَّمَ عَلَى سَيِّدِنَا مُحَمَّدٍ النَّبِيِّ الْأَمِينِ، وَعَلَى آلِهِ وَصَحْبِهِ أَجْمَعِينَ. سُبْحَانَ رَبِّكَ رَبِّ الْعِزَّةِ عَمَّا يَصِفُونَ، وَسَلَامٌ عَلَى الْمُرْسَلِينَ، وَالْحَمْدُ لِلَّهِ رَبِّ الْعَالَمِينَ ۞

## Supplication of Marriage

أَعُوذُ بِاللهِ مِنَ الشَّيْطَانِ الرَّجِيمِ بِسْمِ اللهِ الرَّحْمٰنِ الرَّحِيمِ

اَلْحَمْدُ لِلَّهِ رَبِّ الْعَالَمِينَ وَالْعَاقِبَةُ لِلْمُتَّقِينَ وَالصَّلَاةُ وَالسَّلَامُ عَلَى رَسُولِنَا مُحَمَّدٍ وَعَلَى آلِهِ وَصَحْبِهِ أَجْمَعِينَ اَللَّهُمَّ اجْعَلْ هَذَا الْعَقْدَ مَيْمُونًا وَمُبَارَكًا وَاجْعَلْ بَيْنَهُمَا أُلْفَةً وَمَحَبَّةً وَقَرَارًا وَلَا تَجْعَلْ بَيْنَهُمَا نَفْرَةً وَفِتْنَةً وَفِرَارًا اَللَّهُمَّ أَلِّفْ بَيْنَهُمَا كَمَا أَلَّفْتَ بَيْنَ آدَمَ وَحَوَّاءَ وَكَمَا أَلَّفْتَ بَيْنَ مُحَمَّدٍ وَخَدِيجَةَ الْكُبْرَى وَكَمَا أَلَّفْتَ بَيْنَ عَلِيٍّ وَفَاطِمَةَ الزَّهْرَاءَ اَللَّهُمَّ أَعْطِ لَهُمَا أَوْلَادًا صَالِحًا وَرِزْقًا وَاسِعًا

وَعُمْرًا طَوِيلاً رَبَّنَا هَبْ لَنَا مِنْ اَزْوَاجِنَا وَذُرِّيَّاتِنَا قُرَّةَ اَعْيُنٍ وَجْعَلْنَا لِلْمُتَّقِينَ اِمَامًا رَبَّنَا اٰتِنَا فِي الدُّنْيَا حَسَنَةً وَفِي الْاٰخِرَةِ حَسَنَةً وَقِنَا عَذَابَ النَّارِ

## ASSESSMENT

1. Write down the supplication uttered in the Funeral Prayer.
2. Write down a verse that is customarily recited at the end of sermons.
3. Write down a supplication for food.
4. Write down the Salawat Tafrijiyah.
5. How is a sacrificial animal slaughtered and what supplications are made for it?

# READING TEXTS

## Prophet Adam and Prophet Moses

Prophet Adam and Prophet Moses, may peace be upon them, came across one another and stood face to face. (This meeting took place in the Unseen). Prophet Moses said to Adam: "You are our father, who gave us disappointment and frustration. Because of you we were not allowed to stay in Paradise."

Thereupon, Prophet Adam gave such a response: "You are Moses, who was chosen by Allah, given superiority and the Torah. Despite that, you are blaming me for a thing which was decreed on my behalf forty years before my creation."

Here, the Messenger of Allah stopped and said trice: "Adam excelled Moses!"[30]

Scholars of earlier generations have discussed this issue in detail. A summary is as follows:

As Prophet Adam was the forefather of Moses, he was exceeded by Moses.

Prophet Adam, as well as Prophet Moses, are personalities of different *sharia*s (paths to faithfulness). A blameful thing according to one *sharia* may not be same thing according to another. Therefore, Prophet Adam excelled.

Paradise is not an abode of responsibilities. Yet, this world is a place of obligations and responsibilities. Adam, too, was not responsible, there in Par-

---
[30] *Sahih al-Bukhari*, Qadr, 11; *Sahih Muslim*, Qadr, 13

adise. However, Prophet Moses judged his actions according to the principles of this world. Because of this, Prophet Adam is accepted to be the more excelled one.

Here the truth is that Prophet Adam merely wanted to elucidate that everything, be good or evil, is created by Allah the Almighty (the creation of evil is not evil; doing an evil act is evil). That is why he is considered to be more excelled...

Because of respect to our predecessors we will not criticize them. Yet, we would like to underline a subtle wisdom hidden in the sacred words of our Prophet.

Once more, this *hadith* explains to us a secret matter concerning the Divine destiny. The predestination of everything was composed long before the creation.

Secondly, he compared Prophet Adam's words to those of Prophet Moses, and later emphasized Adam's exceeding Moses.

In the following words of the Prophet: "Adam excelled Moses" does not mean that Moses had a wrong perspective of things. For, he drew everyone's attention to Adam's possessing a more comprehensive consideration of matters.

There are two aspects of destiny. The first one is that everything is known, determined, assigned and predestined by Allah the Almighty. This is an aspect of destiny which is controlled by Allah. The second aspect has to do with a person's free will.

Taking into consideration the second aspect of destiny, Prophet Moses assessed the event of Adam's being sent away from Paradise. Whereas, Adam took into consideration the first *and* second aspects of destiny, and spoke after considering both of those positions.

Because of considering the matter in such a way, he is known to have exceeded Moses.

Due to condition of its creation, human free will can provide recourse for mistakes, even though it has no substantial existence. The meaning of the following verse dictates to us this rule: *"(O human being!) Whatever good happens to you, it is from Allah; and whatever evil befalls you, it is from yourself"* (an-Nisa 4:79). However, on the other side of a matter there is a Divine Will. We cannot will anything unless Allah the Almighty wills it, too. *"You cannot will unless Allah wills. Surely Allah is All-Knowing, All-Wise"* (al-Insan 76:30). This verse, too, gives us that lesson.

Allah is the Absolute Ruler, Who can turn down the wills of everyone and decree His own Will.

The following is a good way to think of free will: Envision free will as a spoonful of water, the purpose of which will be known only after it is being added into the ocean. In fact, that spoon on its own is nothing; however, Allah the Almighty, glorified and exalted be He, built the entire Universe upon such a tiny thing. Thereat, a tiny thing is as precious as the entire Universe.

One needs to be quite comprehensive when considering matters of destiny. This comprehensive view represents all positions and degrees.

## The First Sermon

The Preacher of Humankind, peace and blessings be upon him, ascended a pulpit built in Quba and was about to speak to his community. It was his first sermon in Medina. First of all, he praised his Lord, and glorified Him by saying that He has no deficiencies, and then complimented Him with words full of praise. Later on, he turned to the community and uttered the following words:

> "O People! Do invest for yourselves on behalf of the coming Hereafter! Tomorrow you will be able to see them all. I swear by Allah, each of you comes to his senses, leaves his herd without a shepherd and meets with his Lord, then Allah the Almighty, glorified and exalted be He, is going to ask you questions without any interpreter or veil: "Hadn't I sent you a Messenger for communicating the message? Hadn't I given you wealth and gathered it before you? Good, if so, then what have you invested for this day?" The addressee of these words would first look on his right, and then on his left in search; however, he would not find a single thing to hold to. Then, he would look ahead, where he'd see Hellfire with all its horror. Each of you must surely protect himself from the Fire even with a half a date! And if you do not possess that

then you should say a good word! For each and every kind of goodness, committed here, there will be given rewards for ten times more, which will be enough for ascending seven hundred levels above. May Allah's grace and mercy be upon you!"

This oration comprised the first section of the sermon. After sitting for a while on the pulpit, the Messenger of Allah stood up and continued:

"Undoubtedly, all the praise is for Allah the Almighty. I, too, praise Him and ask help from Him, too. We take refuge in Him from the evil of our carnal souls. We also take refuge to His mercy against the evil of our deeds. Surely, no one to whom guidance is given can be misled, just as one whose heart is closed and acts heedlessly cannot keep to the right path. I bear witness that there is no deity other than Allah. He is the only One. He has no companions. The Book of Allah bears the most beautiful words ever. Undoubtedly, after disbelief, Allah had bestowed faith to everyone. The one, who filled his heart with the light of faith and was granted with the perpetual words of the Lord instead of the alluring words of people, is considered to having been saved (from Hell). There is no doubt that the Word of Allah is the most beautiful and the most harmonious word. Do love, beloved people of Allah, and fill your hearts with Divine Love. Do not get bored with Divine Words and do not keep yourselves away from remembrance of Allah in order your hearts not to be left alone with sternness. For, Allah the Almighty, glorified and exalted be He, chose only some among His other creatures! Allah communicated to us the best of deeds and put them before us, assigned guides among His servants, and declared the most beautiful and righteous of words. Everything that is given to humans, those things allowed and forbidden by religion become perceptible, so that nothing remains unrevealed.

Come and join the contest of servitude and never, ever associate companions to Allah the Almighty. Do imbue yourselves with reverence, soar with the hope of taking refuge in Allah's mercy and tremble against His punishment! Do prove your loyalty in the presence of Allah with the most righteous of your words! Do increase love among yourselves with Allah's mercy and benevolence! Undoubtedly, Allah, glorified and exalted be He, will not be contented if people do not fulfill His will. Instead, He will dislike them. May Allah's greetings be upon you all!"[31]

---

[31] *Ibn Hisham*, Sira, 3:30, 31

# REFERENCES

Baltaş, Zuhal and Acar Baltaş, *Bedenin Dili*, İstanbul: Remzi Kitabevi, 2000

Çakan, İ. Lütfi, *Dinî Hitabet*, İstanbul: M. Ü. İlahiyat Fak. Yay., 2007

Çalışlar, Aziz, *Tiyatro Ansiklopedisi*, Ankara: T.C. Kültür Bakanlığı Yay., 1995

Çetin, Abdurrahman, *Hitabet ve İrşad*, Bursa: Aksa Yay., 1998

Gülen, M. Fethullah, *Beyan*, İstanbul: Nil Yay., 2008

Gülen, M. Fethullah, *İrşad Ekseni*, İzmir: Nil Yay., 2002

*İlmihal I-II*, Ankara: Türkiye Diyanet Vakfı, 2004

*İslam Ansiklopedisi*, The articles: "Bayram, Hatim, Hitabet, Hutbe, Mukabele, İmam" Türkiye Diyanet Vakfı

Kasım, Metin, "Spiker Olmak O Kadar Kolay mı?", *Türkiyat Araştırmaları Dergisi*, Issue: 25, Spring 2009